# What people say about James Dillehay's books:

*"Should be viewed as the blueprint for success in the crafts industry."*

The Crafts Report

*"One of the most user-friendly yet practical books of its kind."*

FiberArts Magazine

*"Quite an expert....Very informative. I wish we could keep you for the next three days."*

Carol Duvall, HGTV, The Carol Duvall Show

*"James is by far the most qualified and talented marketer for the craft industry. His knowledge is only outweighed by his honest desire to help people."*

Phoebe Welburn, Vice President, Welburn Gourd Farm

*"A useful and enlightening resource."*

Shuttle Spindle & Dyepot

*"Invaluable, and not just for weavers alone."*

The Bookwatch

*"Since reading James Dillehay's books, I have implemented many of the ideas . . . have sold about 4 times what I sold in the equivalent time last year."*

Julie Anderson, Costume Salon

*"Dillehay knows the field -- I can't think of a more rewarding retirement pursuit."*

Jack Smith, Syndicated Columnist: Senior Sense

*"Everything you need to know is here, and it's applicable to any craft."*

Millennium Whole Earth Catalog

*"This new book is so useful, we can hardly stop using it long enough to review it. If you're considering establishing or improving a web presence, invest in this book."*
The Crafts Fair Guide

*"An excellent book. The appendices guarantee that the book will long remain as a valued resource."*
Charles Jermy, Dean, Cornell University

*"A very useful book for weavers and other craft artists who need solid business information. Recommended for public libraries."*
Library Journal

*"First bit of sanity I've encountered since I began my business. It teaches me everything I need to know, over and over!"*
Carole Baylus, Owing Mills, MD

*" Includes material other books lack. For example, I liked his chapter on 'How to Avoid Becoming a Starving Fiber Artist' in which he discusses grants and funding, exhibitions, competitions and more."*
Crafts Magazine

*"Dillehay knows of what he writes because he's done it. A very handy and practical book."*
Crafts N Things

*"After reading James Dillehay s books, my business took on a new life. My first order was triple what I had planned for, and other orders are pouring in! Because of the techniques I learned from him, my business is thriving."*
Cathy Marble, Chamisa Hill Designs

*"Just what you need; he's clearly been there."*
Weavers Magazine

*"I sold 12 times my booth fee, partly because my stuff is good, but partly because I really researched presentation in James Dillehay's books."*
Joann Wheeler

# STITCH
## for
# CASH

How to Make Money from
Your Knitting, Crochet,
Sewing, Needlearts and
Textile Crafts

JAMES DILLEHAY

# *Stitch for Cash*

ISBN: 978-1-7320264-5-2
Warm Snow Publishers
PO Box 170
Torreon, NM 87061
Craftmarketer.com

**Other books by the author:**
- *How to Price Crafts and Things You Make to Sell*
- *Guerrilla Marketing for Direct Selling* (co-author)

# TABLE OF CONTENTS

Stay informed about what's trending now and
what's coming in the world of marketing your
handmade products. Subscribe at:
**Craftmarketer.com/newsletter/**

# Introduction

You love knitting, crochet, and needlecrafts. You have wondered if you could make money doing what you love. The answer is yes. And this book teaches you how to make that happen.

It gives you ways to turn your passion for crafting textiles from knitting, crochet, sewing, and other needlecrafts into multiple income streams.

For years, I have made money selling my fiber crafts online, at craft shows, wholesale to stores, and through my gallery-gift shop. The last product line I came out with was a fashion accessory that generated over $137,000 in sales.

The lessons discovered in making all of the above happen are in this guide. The advice here can help you whether you are just starting or if you have already sold some of your pieces and you want to grow.

Growing usually means expanding your product line. You will learn where to find more ideas than you dreamed of, but, more importantly, you will also learn to determine if your concepts will sell in the marketplace.

You will learn how to brand and prepare your product line for prime time; otherwise the later chapters on finding more shoppers to get your message in front of will be a waste of time and money. No amount of marketing can make a weak presentation convert better.

You will discover pricing formulas used by successful sellers that earn you healthy profit margins.

You will get tips for transforming your social connections into customers and ambassadors for your brand.

And you will discover how to find, identify, and pitch your brand to social and media influencers with large followings.

By the end of the book, you will know how to use everything you learn here to scale your handmade venture to as large a business as you can handle.

It's a great feeling when people buy your things and tell you how much they love your work. Getting kudos for your pieces is almost as satisfying as getting paid. Almost. The getting paid part is what keeps the adventure going.

You are about to discover a world of opportunities for growing your indie craft brand. But that doesn't mean you have to be everywhere and do everything all at once. Take baby steps. With experience comes confidence. With confidence comes expansion.

The best place to begin is coming up with ideas for things to make. Let's get profitable from the start by discovering what buyers want and then making your own versions of what's hot in the marketplace.

# CHAPTER 1

# Things to Make and Sell

There are thousands of possibilities of textile and needle crafts to make. This chapter shows you how to find ideas and how to prioritize them by products shoppers want. You will learn:

- How to find product ideas
- How to test-market your indie designed idea to shoppers.
- How to make your product line stand out from others.

\* \* \* \* \*

*Note: the following section reveals how to research markets for product ideas already selling.* ***Do not copy others' work.*** *It's not just unethical; you can lose your online web presence or, worse, be sued for copyright infringement. Use the sources here to brainstorm ideas from which you will craft your own uniquely designed pieces.*

\* \* \* \* \*

## How to Find Product Ideas

Got a product idea and wondering if it's what shoppers are buying? Let's look at how you can use data gathered from buyers on Etsy and Amazon Handmade to learn what consumers are searching for and purchasing.

EtsyRank.com is a subscription service providing reports on keywords used by real buyers on Etsy. Keyword search data changes daily, but as an example of what you can learn are the results from several textile craft-related searches done at the time of this writing using EtsyRank's Keyword Explorer tool:

knit beanies – 1,232 monthly searches
shoulder bag – 3,949 monthly searches
tote bag – 7,979 monthly searches
diaper bag – 4,789 monthly searches
woven basket – 1,857 monthly searches
chunky knit blanket – 6,187 monthly searches
baby girl clothes – 4,371 monthly searches
baby blankets – 3,784 monthly searches
boho clothing – 1,483 monthly searches
mittens – 3,009 monthly searches
festival clothing – 3,162 monthly searches
headbands – 6,177 monthly searches
Christmas decorations – 20,936 monthly searches
ugly holiday sweater – 12,776 monthly searches
teddy bear – 2,073 monthly searches

Those same products were searched for by shoppers on Amazon (results from MerchantWords.com a subscription service):

knit beanies – 5,500 monthly searches
shoulder bag – 1,800 monthly searches
tote bag – 3,500 monthly searches
diaper bag – 115,400 monthly searches
woven basket – 145,700 monthly searches
chunky knit blanket – 57,500 monthly searches
baby girl clothes – 602,100 monthly searches
baby blankets – 145,000 monthly searches
boho clothing – 13,000 monthly searches
mittens – 11,900 monthly searches
festival clothing – 9,200 monthly searches
headbands – 91,000 monthly searches
Christmas decorations – 312,700 monthly searches
ugly holiday sweater – 1,700 monthly searches
teddy bear – 201,800 monthly searches

The search terms above are product related. But that's not the only way to get ideas of popular items to make and sell.

Other search terms can also give you ideas, like the following taken from EtsyRank's Trend Buzz report:

personalized gifts: 439,160 monthly searches
craft kits: 177,477 monthly searches
fall decor: 95,132 monthly searches
wedding gifts: 61,154 monthly searches
bridesmaid gifts: 60,895 monthly searches
anniversary gifts for boyfriend: 38,862 monthly searches
dog collar: 38,248 monthly searches
groomsmen gifts: 31,576 monthly searches
boyfriend gift: 27,302 monthly searches

*Search data changes daily. Sales vary according to the time of year, because some items sell better near the end of year holiday season. Note that Amazon search results include searches for products that are not necessarily handmade.*

The above results are a sampling of what shoppers search for. Learn more about using keyword search tools in the chapter on SEO.

### More Ways to Find Trending Product Ideas

A brainstorming technique that will give you quick results for things to make is to look on Etsy and Amazon. Start with the major categories and expand those into hundreds of subcategories. See: https://www.etsy.com/help/categories/seller.

On Amazon, go to: https://www.amazon.com/Best-Sellers-Handmade/zgbs/handmade/ to view bestsellers in the Handmade category. Not only will you get product ideas from the subcategories themselves, you'll get a look at seller listings that are working well.

From the two steps mentioned, start your own list of subcategories of products you could or want to make. Prioritize your ideas. Pick things you will enjoy making. You can be profitable with just one or two types of products. Later on, add new items as your business grows.

Pick up clues for product ideas from fashion newsletters. See the huge list on Pinterest at: https://www.pinterest.com/aqeelasasman/fashion-newsletters/.

Another source for inspiration is to follow influencers on Instagram who have large audiences. Use the free version plan at Heepsy.com to find influencers by topics, like "style" or "fashion."

## How to Test-Market Your Product Idea

No matter how great you (and your mom) think your ideas are, you can't survive or thrive in the business world without first testing and measuring how the buying public reacts to your handmade products.

The fastest real-life testing ground for handmade products is to post on social sites like Instagram, Pinterest, and Facebook. Post images or videos of your products. Take notes about how your followers react.

Your social media contacts know you, or kind of know you, so they may give you positive encouragement. Many Etsy stores have grown their customer base starting with sales from friends, family, and social media connections.

Another powerful feedback trial is wearing something you've made and walking into several boutiques you think would be a good fit for your style. Start a conversation with a sales clerk or, better yet, the owner. Be bold. Ask what they think. The feedback will be invaluable.

## Ways to Make Your Product Line Stand Out

After you have your product list, the next step is making things. Since there's usually competition, let's look at ways to craft products so they stand out from other sellers. The following list will help:

* **Your story.** Your story is the connecting message. Shoppers want to do business with businesses that care. Telling them your story relates what you care about.

* **Quality sells**. Whatever you make, do it well. Quality work is obvious and attractive. My craft teacher used to say,

"Your handwork doesn't lie. All your mistakes come back to haunt you."

* **Niches**. Breaking into retail with a new line, you face a crowded market. To stand out, look for a low-competition niche area within a category. For example, if you craft handbags, develop a line for young girls instead of bags for all women.

* **Colors**. Next to quality, the colors you use play a major role in standing out over similar but competing products. If you are good (as in: your work is selling) at putting colors together, you have a huge advantage. For those without training in working with color, see the book *Color Works* by Deb Minz.

* **Themes**. Design your product line around a theme. Many of your customers will have someone on their gift list who collects dinosaurs, unicorns, elephants, gnomes, or other collectibles.

* **Personalization**. Personalized gifts are very popular, both at shows and on Etsy. If appropriate for what you make, offer the option to add a recipient's name to an item for a premium price. Some top-selling products on Etsy and Amazon Handmade offer customizing or personalizing as an option.

* **Inform shoppers if you use sustainable materials**. Don't assume customers will know that you are a "green business." Point it out in promotional material like hangtags, packaging, websites, and booth displays.

* **Packaging**. Packaging is another place to brand your business. It's also a way to use sustainable materials (call attention to this on your boxes and wrappers) as many companies that make packaging boxes and bags do so with recycled paper.

* **Eye-catching images**. When listing your products online, your images do the selling (or not.) If there is any place in your business that justifies investing money, it is in getting great photos of your work. See Appendix 1 for resources.

### Sell Sets or Bundles

Selling several items together at a slightly discounted price can be more profitable than focusing on single product sales. A discounted set is a clear savings to shoppers. When you can move more items at one time, you will usually save on costs of sale down the road. Every time you make a sale, whether it's at a craft fair, on Etsy, or anywhere else, there is a cost of sale involved. For instance, booth fees at events, listing and sales fees on Etsy, and so on.

Some crafts lend themselves naturally to package deals. Jewelers often put together sets made up of a bracelet, earrings, and necklace. Knitters make hat and glove sets. The more related the items are, the easier it will be for the customer to see the value in purchasing a set.

Naming your packaged products helps call attention to how the deal is special. Call the product bundle a collector's set, a gift basket, or holiday set, and give each one a name; something like The Artisan's Selection or Your Name's Gift Set.

Bundling can bring you a new world of gift buying customers both individuals looking for something special and businesses and associations that reward employees with performance bonuses. Real estate brokers sometimes send gift baskets to their clients after closing a deal. Gift baskets also allow you to zero in on specific occasions like Christmas, Easter, graduation, Mother's Day, Valentine's and many others.

\* \* \* \* \*

## How Customers Give You Product Ideas

*I designed my scarf line in more than twenty color combinations (yes, I know that seems crazy), but shoppers would sometimes ask for colors I wasn't yet making. Every time I filled one of these special requests, I'd make extras because it was a more efficient use of my time and I wanted to see how the public responded to the new colors. Often, the specially-requested color combo outsold my other designs.*

*Many of my customers mentioned they were buying a scarf as a gift and wanted to tell the recipient how to wear it. So I started including a "how to wear" instruction card to go with each scarf.*

*Since more and more customers were buying gifts, I began packaging and displaying the scarves in a gift box with the "how to wear" card.*

*Important takeaways: Customers told me what they wanted. Tweaking my product offer according to their suggestions increased my sales.*

*I was no longer just in the scarf market, I was also in the gift market. Appealing to gift buyers eventually accounted for nearly half my business growth.*

\* \* \* \* \*

Now that you know the basics for finding ideas to turn into lovely items consumers want, you are one step closer to starting your venture. Next, you will need to get set up to accept payments, choose a catchy business name, and a few other things. Read on for how to get your new business started the right way.

# CHAPTER 2

# Steps for Start Ups

Before you can make sales, you need a couple of things in place. This chapter explains the basic legal requirements for setting up your business to avoid future problems with the IRS and to make your gig operate more smoothly.

Here you will learn about:

- Choosing a name for your business
- Legal requirements: permits and licenses
- Accepting credit card payments
- Keeping records

## Choosing a Name for Your Business

Your business needs a name that is short, catchy, memorable, and doesn't already belong to someone else.

Many makers use their own name as their business name. For one, it's more personal; shoppers can see you are a real person standing behind your name.

Another plus for using your name is that it makes it easy for customers who have bought from you at events to recognize your name when it appears on their receipt and credit card statement. Occasionally, a shopper won't remember all the vendors she bought from and then may later dispute the charge after going over her credit card statement.

If you don't want to use your name, make a list of your favorite alternatives with the best one at the top. Wait a few days for your ideas to settle before reviewing your list. If you still like your choice after time has passed, the next step is to learn if the name is already in use.

A Google search is usually a good place to start. If Google doesn't return a link with your ideal business name, next check for registered trademarks at www.uspto.gov/trademarks/process/search/.

If you don't find your prospective name registered as a trademark, then do a business name search in your state. Do this by searching the phrase "business name availability (your state's name)." Usually, this search will bring up your state's business filings bureau where you can learn if anyone else is already using the name you have in mind.

After you have done the research and confirmed that no one else is already using your ideal business name, register it with a business license.

\* \* \* \* \*

## Necessity and Invention

*Daymond had a hard time in school, his future didn't look bright. Unknown to him at the time, he had dyslexia. To get by, he took a job as a waiter. But he also nurtured a dream of being in business.*

*After explaining what he wanted to do—craft a man's apparel line—his mother showed him how to sew. Armed with his new skill set, he got hold of enough fabric to make eighty caps for men, all of which he sold. He soon had a going business he called FUBU (For Us By Us). It really helped when Daymond managed to get his line placed in popular music videos.*

*FUBU grew, grossing over $300 million in its first six years. FUBU's sales eventually hit over $6 billion. From humble beginnings, Daymond Dohn became a member of the original cast on the reality show for entrepreneurs called Shark Tank.*

*His book,* The Power of Broke, *tells how he leveraged the feelings of being back-against-the-wall poor into creative thinking.*

\* \* \* \* \*

# Legal Requirements: Permits and Licenses

For most businesses that don't sell food or alcohol, there are usually four registrations or permits you need to operate legally in the US:

**Zoning permit waiver**. Most side gigs or small startups will be run from home, which is more than likely in a residential area. Your home probably isn't zoned for doing business. However, you may still be allowed to operate with a zoning waiver as long as your home business activity doesn't draw attention or get complaints from neighbors. Visit your city or county zoning office to learn what's required.

**Local business license**. Apply at your local county business registration office. Locate yours at: sba.gov/business-guide/launch-your-business/apply-licenses-permits.

**State sales tax permit**. In the US, except for Alaska, Delaware, Montana, New Hampshire and Oregon, all states require a state sales tax permit for selling products or services in the respective area. To learn where to get a sales tax permit in your state, do an online search for "(your state name) sales tax permit." Usually the state sales tax permit is free. Once you are signed up, the state will send you forms to fill out and return with any sales tax collected. If you will sell at festivals and art and craft shows, most events require a state sales tax permit.

**Federal Employer Identification Number (EIN).** If your business doesn't have employees, you may not need an EIN. Sole proprietors can use their social security number when reporting business income to the IRS. If you hire others, you'll need the EIN. Apply online at ein-forms-gov.com/.

### Starting a Business outside the US

For starting and registering a business in Canada, see canada.ca/en/services/business/start.html.

For the UK, visit www.gov.uk.

For Australia, start at register.business.gov.au. Also see business.gov.au/registrations/register-for-taxes/tax-registration-for-your-business

Within EU: <u>europa.eu/youreurope/business/running-business/start-ups/starting-business/index_en.htm</u>

For other countries, Google the phrase "how to legally start a business in (insert your country name)."

## Accepting Credit Card Payments

If you sell at trunk shows, home parties, or craft fairs, a mobile credit card reader allows you to accept credit card payments through your mobile phone or notebook.

If you plan to sell on Etsy or Amazon Handmade, you won't need a credit card processor as the site handles transactions and passes on the processing fee to you.

If you have your own website, you will need a credit card processor to handle transactions from online sales.

Does accepting credit cards make a difference? For impulse buys like those at craft shows, the answer is a definite yes. My sales more than doubled when I began accepting cards. I'm not alone. A survey showed 83% of businesses report it increased their sales.

Almost 80% of shoppers prefer using a credit card. Fortunately, technology has made it easy to accept credit cards from just about anywhere. Using a small card reader that plugs into your smartphone and an app from your card processor, you will key in an item, swipe or insert the card, and have the buyer sign with their finger or a stylus pen.

Two popular mobile credit card service providers among craft show vendors are Square at <u>squareup.com</u> and PayPal at <u>paypal.com/us/webapps/mpp/credit-card-reader</u>. Both services allow you to accept credit card payments through your smartphone with no monthly charges and only a per-transaction fee. Money from a sale minus the fee is deposited directly into your checking account.

## Keeping Records / Accounting

Keep records of your sales along with your expenses. The IRS requires businesses to keep records and file income tax, even when you don't show a profit.

There are different ways of keeping records. If you have a smartphone, there are apps like Expensify that allow you to snap photos of your receipts. If you prefer to make entries by hand, log books for tracking expenses can be found at office supply stores and bookstores.

TaxJar integrates with Etsy shops making it easy to record sales data. Other accounting tools include: Wave, QuickBooks Self-Employed, GoDaddy Bookkeeping for Etsy Sellers, and Zoho.

I'm not an affiliate for QuickBooks, but I just love it's ease of use. Since I started working with the online version, my book-keeping has been smooth sailing. It synchronizes my business credit card, checking account, PayPal, and my Etsy store. At any given moment, I can log in and get a snapshot of my finances.

Examples of expenses you may be allowed to deduct from your business income include: business-related insurance, show rental fees, bank charges, trade periodicals, advertising, office supplies, utilities, contract labor, salaries, equipment rentals or repairs, depreciation, and the cost of goods sold.

For more tax advantages from your craft business, see *How to Price Crafts and Things You Make to Sell*.

Once you have an accounting system in place, it's a good practice to back up your files regularly and store them safely. After a computer failed and wiped all my data, I now keep two sets of external hard-drive backups and one online backup account.

\* \* \* \* \*

## Make a Business Out of Helping Other Makers

*Amanda Judge found a purpose and a business in Peru. While working on her master's degree, she saw how local communities in Latin America and other countries around the world could become economically sustainable from their artisan-made products. This gave her the idea to launch Shop-Faire.com, a fair trade accessories business. Her business has created opportunities around the globe, empowering women to flourish and support their families in previously impoverished areas.*

\* \* \* \* \*

## Create a Production Logbook

Keeping a production logbook helps when it comes time to reproduce an item. In my logbook, I include a photo or drawing of each piece with details of material costs, production time, finished dimensions, how well an item sold, and other notes.

Legal and accounting stuff may seem tedious, but doing it right means you can relax and move forward without the worry of future troubles with the government.

Next, let's look at how to brand your messaging to shoppers so you convert more of them from browsers into buyers.

# CHAPTER 3

# Setting Up Your Brand

If you were going on a date and wanted to impress the other person, you would likely take extra steps with grooming and dressing. Likewise, when getting your products ready to market, there are steps for making your line stand out and increase engagement.

This chapter teaches you how to brand your business with your photos, promotional material, and packaging. When selling online or to stores, your presentation has to sell for you.

Promotional material gives you a way to pass along branding cues so customers remember and refer others to you. Branding includes your story and how you message it. It also includes the use of consistent style elements like fonts, colors, and icons that go into your signage, business cards, hangtags, web pages, and more.

## Branding Cues

First impressions are often lasting ones, including brand names and logos. The following elements can help you build your brand's message. Some of these were also mentioned earlier as being important ways to make your product line stand out.

* **Your Story.** People relate to stories. Your story has the potential to pull heartstrings. Mass-manufactured things rarely connect us to real people behind the products. The buy-handmade and sustainable-fashion trends reveal that shoppers are rejecting factory-made products in favor of individual creativity.

* **Your Business Name.** After you've settled on the name you intend to use, place it throughout your promotional material.

* **Your Authenticity.** Large companies have a problem conveying authenticity. Corporations don't have souls. As a

small business, if you are authentic, that's your brand. No one else is like you. All of your choices around logos, fonts, colors, and images can reflect your personality.

* **Images.** Images tell stories. They deliver visuals when you are marketing online and for your display when you are at art or craft shows. You need: product-only images with a white background for online store listings, how-it's-made images, how-it's-used images if needed, lifestyle images showing people enjoying your item, jury images when applying to arts and crafts fairs, and pictures of you to accompany your artist's story. See Appendix 1 for more on photos.

* **Your Logo.** A logo is a small visual that expresses a feeling you want to convey to shoppers. Later in this chapter, you will find where you can design your logo or hire it out to professional graphic designers.

* **Your Elevator Pitch.** In a few short sentences (30 seconds or less to say) what does your product promise customers? For example, a handbag maker promises buyers a "fashion accessory that's practical and stylish."

* **Fonts and Colors.** Consistency is part of good branding. Choose fonts and colors that match your personality and use the same ones on all your printed materials and website content.

* **Your Contact Information.** Every message you send or promote through should contain information on how people can easily reach you, including your website, phone number, e-mail, and address.

When thinking about how to design your brand's look and feel, get inspired by checking out how successful sellers brand their business.

Head over to Craftcount.com and choose the category closest to your product line. Craftcount displays the top-selling Etsy shops.

Also, check out Amazon bestsellers by category at https://www.amazon.com/Best-Sellers/zgbs. Choose "Handmade" for your main category and then drill down into the subcategories closest to yours and Amazon will show you the top sellers in those niches.

\* \* \* \* \*

## Photos Make the Difference Online

*Broke and something of a rebel, Sophia started listing vintage clothing on eBay. Because of her gift for taking photos that matched her customers' life-style cravings, her "Nasty Gal" became an online fashion brand, creating a multimillion-dollar empire. Sophia Amoruso is the author of the best-selling book Girl Boss, which spawned a series on Netflix.*

\* \* \* \* \*

## Types of Promotional Materials

Once you have your branding cues created, repurpose them again and again into your promotional messaging using:

**Videos.** Tell your artist's story with video. Video rules online marketing. Over 70% (and rising) of shoppers say video influenced their purchases. Over 90% of watchers are likely to remember a call to action on a video. Etsy, Amazon, and most social sites encourage product videos to increase sales.

**Business cards** are among the entrepreneur's cheapest yet most useful tools. Imagine you are wearing something you made when someone crosses paths with you and says, "That is so cute, where did you get it?" You are ready with a business card with all your contact information.

**Hangtags.** Every piece you sell should have a hanging tag that gives details about your product: the way you made it, simple instructions for product care when appropriate, and something like the words "handmade by" your name.

**Thank You cards.** With every sale, including a signed Thank You card is a warm, personal touch that customers will appreciate because so many sellers neglect to do it. Include your logo and contact info on the back. Consider offering a discount off the customer's next order.

**Packaging.** Packaging is another opportunity for branding and messaging. Use (and let customers know that you use):

biodegradable packaging, upcycled corrugated cardboard, recycled paper, or other biodegradable organic materials.

**Signs and banners.** If you do craft shows, expos, or trunk shows, use signs and banners. Many office supply stores can take your PDF file and create a sign with foam board backing, lamination and grommet holes for hanging for a reasonable price.

**Postcards** make low-cost reminders to mail to previous customers. Cards can include an eye-catching image on one side and marketing message, name, address, and website on the other side. Postcards can help sell new products and close-outs. Mail cards periodically to your customer list. Send out invitational notecards to your mailing list whenever you will be back in their area to do a show or home party. One side of the card has your latest catchy image. Since there's no envelope to decide about opening, customers have to see your photo.

**Your voice mail message.** If you don't always answer your phone, your voice mail message can communicate a marketing message. Include your website address and perhaps information about an upcoming craft show where you will be displaying. It means updating your message regularly if you do a lot of shows, but it creates the impression of someone who is busy selling.

**Checks, return address labels, sales receipts, gift certificates, order forms, and sticker labels** provide more opportunities to add a logo, website and promo blurb about what you do. When I accept credit cards at art and craft shows, the customer receives an e-mail or text receipt that includes my business name, a photo of me, and contact information so they can easily remember who they made the purchase from.

## Graphic Design Providers

Good design in your marketing materials is as important as good product images. If you want to design your own, the sites here help with easy-to-use templates:

- Canva.com
- GetStencil.com
- Snappa.com

- Fotor.com
- DesignBold.com

Not sure where to start with creating packaging? Find creative examples at:

- Flickr.com/search/?q=packaging
- Pinterest.com (search for "packaging design creative.")

If you don't want to design your own materials, hire graphic designers to do it for you at:

- CreativeMarket.com
- MockupEditor.com
- DesignHill.com
- CrowdSpring.com
- Fiverr.com
- HatchWise.com (logos)
- Etsy.com Search for "logo design" or "banner design" or "etsy shop makeover"

## Printing Services

- VistaPrint.com
- GotPrint.com
- Moo.com
- Printique.com

Preparing your small business for prime time has hopefully gotten you excited about launching your product line. Next in our steps of getting ready for the marketplace, we need to price your crafted items so you make a profit. The next chapter reveals the pricing formula for selling in retail or wholesale and online and off.

# CHAPTER 4

# Pricing for Profit

This chapter teaches you how to price your handmade items so you make a healthy and fair profit. Knowing your profit margins guides your choices in where and what you will sell and how you grow your craft business.

What you will learn:
- Understanding retail and wholesale pricing
- Discovering how much shoppers will pay
- How much it costs you to make an item
- The pricing formula
- Your profit margin

## Understanding Retail and Wholesale Pricing

You may sell your handmade pieces in several markets like on Etsy or Amazon, in gift shops, at home parties, at craft shows and expos, through boutiques, or even mail-order catalogs. These markets fall into one of two categories: retail or wholesale. This section describes the different approaches for pricing in each category.

Retail pricing is the amount you ask for a piece when you are selling direct to a customer. Examples of places you might sell retail include art and craft shows, festivals, online through a website, home parties, or from your own studio.

Wholesale pricing is the amount you charge for items you sell to someone else who resells your products to their customers. For instance, stores, galleries, and mail-order catalogs like *Sundance Catalog* are wholesale markets. Stores price items two to two-and-a-half times what they pay for them.

If you plan to grow your business by selling to stores, knowing your costs and your prices tells you if you can afford to sell wholesale. Imagine having fifty or more stores around the country showing your items five to seven days a week.

There's no definitive answer to whether wholesale or retail is a better business model. I know makers who will not do craft shows, choosing instead to work from home. I know others who only do shows or sell online and never wholesale. And there are other sellers like me who do both.

## How Much Will Shoppers Pay?

The question almost every new maker asks is, "How much should I charge for my work?" For pricing, an even more important question is, "How much will shoppers pay?"

You don't want to lose money by asking only enough to get back your costs when customers will gladly pay higher prices.

To find the average price buyers will pay for pieces like yours, survey what is selling where and for how much. This can be an adventure of sorts, going online to browse Etsy or Handmade on Amazon or visiting craft fairs and stores to scope out the marketplace.

You may find the average market price for an item is higher at one place than it is for similar work in a different market(s). For example, a knitted hat may sell on Etsy at one price, at craft fairs at a different price, and in stores for a higher price.

\* \* \* \* \* \*

## My Introduction to Pricing

*I was finishing my very first scarf when a visitor was walking through the studio where I was working. She oohhed and aahhed over the piece. She asked, "How much do you want for it?" It never occurred to me anyone would buy the thing. It was a practice piece my weaving teacher had given me so I could learn different techniques. Clueless as to its value, I blurted out, "How about thirty-five dollars?" She jumped on it. My asking price was pitifully low. Since that first sale, I've sold similar pieces for $150.*

# Cost of Goods or Production Cost

Cost of goods is what you spend to produce the products you sell. it includes all material, labor, and overhead costs.

### Materials Cost

Your materials may include fabric, yarn, thread, elastic, trims, ribbons, glue, dye, or other supplies. Regardless of how little you use, it's important to include the costs of everything that goes into making each piece. Don't neglect to add any shipping charges and sales tax you paid for materials shipped to you.

As an example, say you make a woman's clutch:

Cost of materials (not counting preparation): $3
Zipper, liner, thread and miscellaneous supplies: $4.25
Total materials cost: $7.25

### Labor Cost

Cost of labor is the dollar value of the time needed to gather, prepare and produce an item. If you make all your products yourself, your cost of labor will be the hourly wage you pay yourself or others you hire.

When starting out, make a few pieces first to learn realistically just how many hours you (or your workers) take to complete an item. Once you are up to what will be your average working speed, clock yourself making a single item.

How much is your time worth? This is something you have to decide, but a good starting amount is $20 per hour.

If you can sell items at a price that would pay you $30, $35, or more per hour, you can profitably hire others at a lower rate (like $15 per hour) to help produce your pieces when sales justify outsourcing labor.

Continuing with the example of the clutch, let's say you decided that you value your labor at $20 per hour.

Time to arrange materials before assembly: 2 min
Time to sew and finish one clutch: 13 min
Total cost of labor: .25 hours (15 minutes) x $20 per hour = $5

*Note: when you make a piece for the first time, your labor time will be longer. After making several, you will have learned ways to cut the production time. With practice, you'll arrive at the true cost of your labor.*

Up to now, you have calculated the cost of materials for the clutch at $7.25 and the labor at $5, bringing your costs to $12.25. We now need to account for another, often overlooked cost of doing business commonly known as overhead.

### Overhead Cost

Overhead refers to expenses you pay to operate your business day-to-day, even if you work from home. Overhead is also referred to as fixed costs because these expenses remain in a predictable range throughout the year, regardless of how much you sell.

Examples of overhead include: business licenses, rent, utilities, phone, insurance, advertising, office supplies, cleaning supplies, professional dues, and so on.

Calculating all those costs would take time. More established businesses will do the due diligence, but an easy shortcut for a home business is to figure 25 percent of the total of your materials and labor costs to arrive at a number that approximates your overhead.

Adding estimated overhead costs for clutch:
$5 labor + $7.25 materials = $12.25
$12.25 x 25% estimated overhead = $3.07

Total production cost for clutch:

$12.25 + $3.07 = $15.32

## The Pricing Formula

As you can see in the example above, the total of labor, materials and overhead for making one clutch is $15.32. This is the amount we have to recover to break even. But $15.32 isn't necessarily what you would price the clutch at.

Go back to the research you did earlier to learn the average market price for similar clutches. You may find those like yours sell on Etsy or Amazon or at crafts fairs for an average price of $20 or more. Since that's a price that shoppers are used to seeing, you would be in line to price yours at least $20.

## Calculating Wholesale Prices

Let's say clutches like yours sell in boutiques for $30. Shops mark up items two to two and half times to arrive at their retail price. In this instance, the shop will only pay $12 to $15 per clutch.

You have a problem because your break-even cost is $15.32. You would lose money selling wholesale. In a case like this, one needs to:

- Lower material or labor costs, and / or
- Enhance the perceived value of the clutches so the store owner will bump up the retail, or
- Choose other items to make that are profitable to sell wholesale.

## What's Your Profit Margin?

One of the most important things to learn early on in your business is your profit margin. This amount is the difference between your cost of goods and your asking price. Your profit margin will differ depending on whether you sell retail or wholesale.

If your cost of goods is $10 and your retail price is $30, your profit margin is $20. If your cost of goods is $10 and your wholesale price is $14, your profit margin is $4.

Use the free Craftmarketer.com/pricing-calculator/
to determine your profit margins and prices.

Knowing profit margins enables you to make choices for growth by telling you:

- If you can afford to offer free shipping, which will increase your sales.
- If you can afford to hire help with production, which will allow you to produce more inventory.
- How much money you can spend on ads.
- If you can profitably sell wholesale to stores where you can scale up your business by adding more and more accounts.

\* \* \* \* \* \*

## Helping Military Families

*As military spouses, Lisa Bradley and Cameron Cruse found they shared a common problem—employment struggles when forced to move as their husbands got transferred to different bases. They needed flexible, mobile income.*

*The two created R. Riveter bags, apparel and accessories fashioned from up-cycled canvas Army tents and deer hide leather. Every product is made by hand by military spouses.*

*In 2016, Cameron and Lisa pitched their vision on Shark Tank, earning them a partner / investor relationship from billionaire Mark Cuban. R. Riveter bags and their mission has been featured on CNN, HLN, Martha Stewart American Made, Fox News, MSNBC, Forbes, Inc. 500 and many more.*

\* \* \* \* \* \*

Pricing correctly is one of the key fundamentals in growing a business. Please, please, please don't neglect to calculate your real costs.

With all the preparations you have done so far, you are ready to map out where, when, and how you will get your fashion crafts in front of buyers. The next chapter shows you how to schedule your marketing action steps.

# CHAPTER 5

# Your Marketing Plan

With so many possible ways to sell your needlecrafts, it helps to map out your promotional actions day by day, using a marketing calendar or daily planner. With a map and a schedule, you never have to wonder what to do next.

To schedule your marketing communications, you need a list of actions to take. Start with the possibilities extracted from this book. They won't all be appropriate for you, but circle those that are so you can add them to your calendar or planner. You will develop your own ideas as you grow in experience. Add your tactics to the list and to your calendar.

\* \* \* \* \* \*

## What Is Marketing?

*The word marketing is often used interchangeably with advertising. Though advertising is a marketing tactic, it is only one of many. Not all marketing costs money.*

*Here's what marketing is; it is every communication you make about your product, yourself, or your products.*

*It's how you describe what you do, how you dress, your business card, your product packaging, the colors you choose for your logo, and a lot more.*

\* \* \* \* \* \*

# 101 Marketing Ideas

The following suggested actions, grouped by topics, are available as a checklist you can add your own ideas to. This list is a summary for reference. The ideas are explained more fully throughout this book. Download the list at: Craftmarketer.com/book-resources/.

*MAKING PRODUCTS*
Research products in demand
Write your story
Make quality products
Design using colors that sell
Create products using themes
Personalize products
Promote your sustainability
Use recycled packaging material

*PHOTOS & VIDEOS*
Take lots of attractive photos
Product images with white background
How-it's-made images & videos
How-it's-used images & videos
Lifestyle images
Jury images for art & craft shows
Headshot images of you
Behind-the-scenes videos

*BIZ STARTUP*
Choose a catchy business name
Register for a business license
Get set up to accept credit cards
Set up accounting system

*PRE-MARKETING*
Find your authentic voice
Design logo
Elevator pitch

Choose your fonts and colors
Add your contact info
Business cards
Hangtags
Thank you cards
Signs and banners for events
Postcards
Voice mail message
Branding on all stationery

*PRICING*
Average prices for similar work?
Your production cost
Your profit margin
Can you lower your costs?

*SELL AT EVENTS*
Research craft shows, events
Apply to shows
Build attractive display
Get pop-up tent
Make a checklist for doing shows

*SEO - SEARCH ENGINE OPTIMIZATION*
Use EtsyRank or MerchantWords to find keywords
Use keywords in social posts
Use keywords in product listings
Get inbound links

*SELL ON ETSY*
Set up new Etsy shop, or
Get critique of Etsy shop
List products
Keywords in title, tags, descriptions
Add 10 images per listing
Connect Etsy to social media
Test Etsy Promoted Listings
Increase number of listings

Market Etsy store offline
Offer free shipping if possible

ALTERNATIVES TO ETSY
List on Amazon Handmade
List on other Etsy alternatives
Set up your own domain site
WordPress plugin for Etsy Store
Test ads on social media sites

BLOGGING
Set up blog about your niche
Optimize blog posts for SEO
Syndicate posts to social media

SOCIAL MEDIA
Post at least once a day or more
Post with video for engagement
Posts: educate, entertain, inspire
Post links to your products
Schedule posting using apps
Research popular hashtags
Post on Facebook
Post to Instagram
Tweet to Twitter
Pin to Pinterest boards
Get social followers' e-mails

SELL WHOLESALE
Determine production capacity
Costs = 25% or less of the retail price
Professional presentation
Find store buyers using LinkedIn
List on Faire, Tundra, Indieme, WholesaleInABox
Offer online ordering for stores

FREE PUBLICITY
Prepare online media kit

Identify influencers with Heepsy
Use Twitter to find reporters
USNPL lists newspaper writers
Create brief pitch to media
Link to full press release

CUSTOMER MAILING LIST
Set up e-mail management app like Aweber or Mailchimp
Ask customers to give e-mail
Schedule follow-up calendar

MISCELLANEOUS
Track and measure all actions
Listen to what shoppers tell you
Answer all inquiries quickly
Personalize communications
Treat customers fabulously
Make stuff you love making

\* \* \* \* \* \*

## Think Big Even If Your Product Is Small

*With the help of his mother and grandmother, Moziah Bridges started hand making bow ties because he couldn't find ones that fit his personal style. At 12 years old, he went on Shark Tank and wowed the judges, especially Daymond John. Daymond offered to mentor Mozian who went on to make Mo's Bows a global fashion brand.*

\* \* \* \* \* \*

## Daily Planner / Marketing Calendar

After you identify which action steps you want to work with, use a calendar to organize and schedule them. A planner / marketing calendar protects you from getting lost by mapping a direction. It shows you the big picture.

Your calendar helps you avoid costly shotgun marketing and engage in laser-focused, profitable actions you can track and measure.

Now that you have a plan and a calendar of steps to take, you may be wondering about the fastest way to start making sales. For most sellers that's craft shows, expos, and events, described next.

# CHAPTER 6

# Selling at Craft Shows, Expos, and Events

Craft fairs, festivals, and consumer expos attract thousands of shoppers who buy handmade items. Craft shows are a great venue for testing your products to learn how shoppers react. Events can also be a fast way to put cash in your wallet.

Shows and events don't require a huge commitment. You can do one or two events, feel the pulse of the market for your product line, and then go on to other events.

Selling at shows has challenges. Events can be physically and energetically taxing. At a busy show, you may talk to hundreds of shoppers about your products and your process.

With so many events happening year round, it's important to choose the right ones for your work. The better-attended shows require vendors to pay for booth rental fees six months or longer in advance of the event. The top shows are highly competitive because they historically perform well for sellers.

Discover if selling at fairs and events is for you. Here we cover:

- Types of events
- Where to find events
- How much shows cost you
- How much you can earn
- How to apply
- Displaying your products
- Accepting credit cards

- Checklist for preparing
- More tips for having great shows

## Types of Events

Events and shows that hand-makers display their work at include:

**Craft shows.** Art and craft shows can be juried or not. Juried means you apply with images of your work and judges decide to accept or reject your application. Jurying (ideally) weeds out vendors selling imported products that are not hand-made.

**Juried shows** are often annual events with a history of good attendance. Examples of annual juried art and craft shows that draw hundreds of thousands of visitors include: Plaza Art Fair in Kansas City; Rio Grande Arts and Crafts Fair Balloon Festival in Albuquerque; One-of-a-Kind Holiday Show in Chicago; Tempe Festival of the Arts in the Phoenix area; and Bayou City Art Festival in Houston.

**Local fashion shows.** Fashion shows are held several times a year in most large cities. Often, a local chamber of commerce will sponsor or promote these events. Fashion shows attract the press and people in your community who are in the business, like boutique owners, style reporters, and other influencers. Though local fashion shows may not result in a lot of cash sales, they are a way to connect with the movers and shakers in your area. Find them by googling "fashion shows in (your town)."

**Trunk shows.** Partner with local boutiques by getting them to host a trunk show for your product line. If they mail their list about it, you can expect to be very busy during the event. If you aren't already selling to the shop, you'll make an arrangement to split the sales, probably 50/50. Trunk shows are a great way to get your product line in the door of a boutique you want to be selling your work.

**High-end flea markets.** If you make low-priced items like earrings, bracelets, etc., consider trying a popular flea market if there's one local to you. One of the most well-known is First

Monday in Canton, Texas, attracting over 250,000 visitors each month.

After years of displaying at different kinds of events, both winners and losers, I urge caution when considering:

**First-time events.** Avoid events that are new. First-time shows have not built a following so attendance can be poor to non-existent. Be on your guard with event promoters who approach you at a show attempting to sell you on applying to their upcoming event. They will tell you how great their show is and how their vendors are all happy with their sales. Reality check. If their show was as good as they make it out to be, they wouldn't need to look for vendors. The better shows always get more applicants than there are available booth spaces.

\* \* \* \* \* \*

## Get in Front of the Crowd

*It's tempting to be swayed by others when you go to start your business. Heck, there are times when you will go looking for advice. Sometimes, though, it's about trying an unconventional path. Jac Vanek grew a huge following through blogging. Her breakout line of rubber bracelets found success at music festivals where she found odd jobs that got her in front of crowds who liked her bracelets. Fast forward to jacvanek.com; Jac has built a brand that sells tees, clothing, and accessories worn by the likes of Miley Cyrus and Demi Lovato.*

\* \* \* \* \* \*

## Finding Events

How do you find the good craft shows, festivals and expos where you can expect decent sales? Find events (sometimes with vendor reviews) online at:

- zapplication.org
- art-linx.com
- artfaircalendar.com
- festivalnet.com

Announcements of shows also appear in magazines and websites for different craft media. *Sunshine Artist* and *Handmade Business* list shows, sales and attendance figures of the bigger art and craft shows.

## Questions to Answer before Applying for Events

* Is the show well known? How many years has it been held?

* Does the promoter advertise in the newspapers, on the radio, billboards, or TV? Better shows are well-promoted each year. The public knows about them and returns faithfully to see what's new.

* How many booth spaces are available for the whole show? A show with 500 booths will draw bigger crowds than a show with only fifty.

* What is the booth rental fee? Is there an extra fee for corner spaces? Usually there is because corners are better selling locations.

* Is there a jury fee? Popular shows charge a separate fee just for applying. The application fee isn't returned if you are rejected, nor is it deducted from your booth fee if you are accepted.

* What size spaces are available? The typical size is 10' x 10' and that is the most common pop-up canopy tent size available.

* Is the event restricted to handmade items?

* Is the show outdoors or inside? If outdoors, what has the weather historically been like at that time of year?

* If the show is outdoors, is it held on streets, sidewalks, parking lots, or a grassy area? Most streets are not level, requiring you to adjust your booth display.

* What are the hours of the event? Most shows require

someone to be in your booth throughout the show hours.

* Is booth setup allowed the day before? If you get into a show where this is the case, take advantage of it.

* How is vendor loading and unloading organized?

* How far away is vendor parking?

* What are the security arrangements? Well-organized out-door events provide security overnight. When you purchase your pop-up tent, get one with side panels so you can zip up the walls.

## What Shows Cost

Show expenses include:

* Jury application fees for the more competitive events (non-refundable even if you are not accepted)

* Booth space rental (usually 10' x 10')

* Travel costs: gas, motel, meals, parking fees

* Your display (grid walls or artist pro-panels, tables)

* Pop-up canopy with side walls

* Weights (to keep your tent from blowing away)

Vendor rental fees at art and craft shows range from $25 a day to $1,000 for a weekend. Local events, like those sponsored by a high school, church or community center, can be inexpensive and easier to get accepted in. Small local events will cost less because you won't have to spend money on travel.

Big-city, popular juried shows charge higher booth-rental fees. They get more applicants than there are available spaces. The sales potential of well-attended shows can be good (but not guaranteed) so traveling to a neighboring state may be worth the added costs.

## How Much Can You Earn?

Unfortunately, it's impossible to estimate your potential earnings from shows without doing them and measuring the results for yourself.

I've been in shows where I sold nothing. When this happens, I don't go back the next year. On the other end of the spectrum, one event brought in over $10,000 in sales over a three-day period. I returned to the show year after year with great results but did not reach that number again. (I originally found the event by googling "top craft shows in the US").

Other sellers I met at different shows told me they did not do well at the same event that was great for me. If I had talked to them before I experienced my fantastic weekend, I might never have tried it. You cannot rely on what I or other vendors tell you about their earnings from shows. Their success doesn't prove the same event will do well for your product line. Sure, it's an indicator, but you can only really know from doing the show yourself.

The best advice I can give you about events is to walk through a show you think might be good for your work and observe how busy the other vendors are. If they are actively selling, then consider applying for the event the following year.

## How to Apply

Most shows and fairs require vendors to fill out an application, either online or via a mailed-in form. Zapplication.org lets you apply to and pay for multiple shows from one website. For the more competitive shows, vendor applications are often due six months to a year before the actual show date.

## Jury Images

If applying for the more competitive events, it may be worth the investment to hire a photographer experienced in art or craft images for juried shows. If you can't afford a photographer and have to take your own photos, see the examples at: http://bermangraphics.com/digital-jury-resources/fixing-jury-images.htm.

## Booth Location

You can't always choose your booth location, but, when possible, take advantage of the opportunity. If you have exhibited at an event in the past, managers may give you the same location you had before or at least give your booth preference a higher priority.

Corner locations (extra fee) can be better because they allow you to open up to traffic flow from two sides.

Getting a booth space near a main walkway close to the show's main entrance will probably be a better location than at the back of the event. Though at well-attended shows, there are no bad locations.

Avoid getting a space near food vendors or entertainment. Food is the top seller at shows and not only are you competing for attention, you must deal with junk food being carried in and around your work. Noise from the entertainment can prevent you from being able to talk to your customers pleasantly. If you don't like your allotted space, ask the show manager before you set up if you can move.

## Displaying Your Products

Your booth should be inviting for customers to walk in and look around. Build your display at home first, and play with variations of how the arrangement looks with your pieces displayed.

Design the layout of your booth to be flexible. Build it so you can set up at least two ways:

- First arrangement for a booth location within a row of booths, set up with three side walls and opening in front for visitors to enter.
- Second arrangement for corner location has two side walls in back and two open sides for visitor traffic coming from two directions.

There are lots of possibilities for setting up your display. I rearranged my display from show to show until I came up with a display that worked best for attracting shoppers.

For ideas for booth displays, see:

- pinterest.com/lifethriftylane/craft-show-display-ideas/
- pinterest.com/junqdiva/diy-craft-show-display-and-set-up-ideas/
- pinterest.com/dillydally/craft-show-booth-inspiration/

A general rule in retail: the fuller your display the more you will sell. Studies show shoppers buy more from a full rack or table.

Keep your display racks and tables neat during the entire show. It may mean going over to straighten merchandise many times during the day.

## Pop-Up Canopy Tent

* For outdoor events, you need protection from sun and weather. A pop-up canopy will adequately protect you and your pieces.

* Physical safety of your customers, fellow vendors, and your merchandise should be a priority in constructing your booth. Frame and covers should be sturdy enough to withstand high winds, rain, and large crowds.

* Bring weights to attach to your pop-up tent. Weights keep your tent from blowing into your neighbor's display.

* White tarps work best with pop-up tents. Colored tarps cast a hue on your merchandise.

* Get a pop-up tent you can quickly set up and easily break down for transport. You want to be able to quickly set up your tent and break it down at the end of the event.

* KD canopy and EZ Up have been making pop-up tents for art and craft fairs for many years. Check Craigslist or eBay for deals. Search for "canopy tent" or "ez up tent" or "pop-up tent".

## Accept Credit Cards

As mentioned earlier, being able to accept credit cards will help your sales, especially at art and craft shows. Mobile phone card readers make it easy to process sales quickly. Credit card purchases can increase your overall sales by 30% to 40%.

* * * * * *

### Sell Your Message

*Brothers John and Bert sold T-shirts as they lived out of their van. They sold on the streets, college campuses, and wherever else they could. They got by, barely.*

*Then one of their designs with the words "Life is Good" took off. Seeing it as a clue, they rebranded their business based on that slogan.*

*Their mission wasn't selling their clothing line, it was spreading good vibes. Does selling a positive outlook pay? It did for the Jacobs brothers. Life is Good is a million-dollar global brand.*

*Their success allowed them to help kids for whom life hasn't been so good by creating the Life is Good Playmakers Foundation. See more at: lifeisgood.com.*

\* \* \* \* \* \*

## More Tips for Successful Shows

* Show up to events early. You never know how setup will go with many vendors arriving at the same time—all in a hurry to get their displays up.

* Bring a small folding table to carry out sales transactions. This will be where the customer can comfortably write a check or sign for a credit card sale. Keep extra pens around.

* Make it easy for customers to buy. Have all the materials you need to complete a sale nearby, including: receipt book, brochures, business cards, price lists, and bags or boxes for packaging sales.

* Have a receipt book for customers who want a written receipt. It also makes a great excuse to get the customer's address.

* Ask customers to get on your mailing list. If they don't buy at the show, they may purchase your work later.

* Have a supply of artist statements, bookmarks, business cards or postcards about you and your work to give with each sale or inquiry.

* For indoor events, consider buying a carpet remnant or rug for your booth. It looks good and gives you and your customers some relief from concrete floors.

* Make price signs or price tags. You will tire of answering the question, "How much is it?"

* For makers of wearables, wear something you have made; be a walking ad for your work.

* If you have won competitions, post your awards.

* Bring your own food. It lessens your time away from your booth during the busy part of the day.

* Keep notes about shows by name, city, travel distance, costs, crowd size, weather, parking, layout, sales, and other notes to yourself.

* Shows can be both exciting and demanding. Hundreds, possibly thousands of potential customers come by your booth, many of whom will look at your work and talk to you briefly. It helps if a friend or family member can assist you. At some point, you will want to take a break.

\* \* \* \* \* \*

## Make and Take

*You have probably heard of craft studios you can walk into, create a handmade product, and take it home with you. Creme de la Craft took that idea to a whole other level.*

*Founder Natalie Pirveysian, a passionate DIY-er, teaches craft classes at private parties and organizations' events. She matches craft projects with an event's theme.*

*Natalie offers DIY craft projects that can be "upcycled" from everyday objects found around the home, from cereal box notebooks to milk jug containers.*

*Natalie's business ballooned after being featured in magazines like Ladies' Home Journal, shopping blogs and websites including: Oprah Winfrey Network, The Huffington Post, Buzzfeed, The Washington Post and Babble.*

*Could you do something similar with your skills?*

\* \* \* \* \* \*

Events let you meet people, make sales, and add new names to your customer list. Not everyone will buy at an event, but they may take your card or agree to be on your mailing list. Read how to take advantage of your customer list in Chapter 15.

At almost every event I display at, within days afterwards, I get orders on my Etsy store from someone who saw my pieces at the show but for whatever reason did not buy then.

Though meeting customers at events is probably the fastest way to market your products—cool handmade stuff practically sells itself—you may prefer to stay home and sell online. The coming chapters give you tools and resources for growing sales online. The first step is understanding SEO or Search Engine Optimization.

# CHAPTER 7

# SEO – How Buyers Search Online

S EO—or search engine optimization—refers to using techniques to improve a web page's likelihood of showing up in search results for specific search terms or keywords.

If your product listing, blog post or YouTube video shows up on the first page for a search, it brings you free, organic traffic. There aren't many ways to market for free, but SEO is probably the closest to free you will find.

When you think of search engines, Google, Bing, or Yahoo may come to mind. But Etsy, Amazon, and eBay are also search engines, in addition to being huge marketplaces with shopping carts.

The factors that go into how e-commerce search engines rank one page over another for specific keyword searches change frequently as sites evolve toward creating relevant results for users. But there are elements that consistently influence search rankings, which you will discover in the following topics:

- Finding search terms buyers use
- Keyword tools
- Inbound links to your pages
- Engagement
- Where to place keywords and tags

Search is powerful. It has driven the boom of e-commerce both through computers and more and more on mobile devices. Eighty-seven percent of people using a smartphone search online at least once a day.

People search online for solutions to their problems. They search for opportunities. They search for entertainment. They search to learn. More important to you, they search for hand-made and stylish products to buy.

## Finding Search Terms Buyers Use

You have probably come across the following words: tags, keywords, and search terms. For our purposes, they refer to the same thing. They are the words and phrases people type in a search bar to find what they need online.

In order for your product pages to show up in search re-sults, you must include popular and relevant search terms used by shoppers. If you don't use popular search terms on your pages, for the most part, your items won't get found.

*Example of SEO*

The simplest way to explain how SEO works is to show you an example. Let's say your primary craft skill is knitting or crochet and you are looking for ideas about what to make to sell. You are not sure about how buyers look for items like yours, so you want to research items that are "knitted."

In Chapter 1, we learned about a keyword research tool for Etsy called EtsyRank. Typing in "knitted" at EtsyRank.com's keyword tool reveals:

knitted hats – searched for 1,528 times in 30 days
knitted blanket – 1,386 searches
handmade knitted tops – 767 searches
knitted dog sweater – 759 searches
knitted baby blanket – 522 searches
knitted sweater – 441 searches
knitted scarf – 431 searches
organic baby blanket handmade knitted – 390 searches
crocheted or knitted leg warmers – 376 searches
knitted christmas stocking – 318 searches
knitted mug cozy – 309 searches
knitted vest – 299 searches

From the above list, you can see the demand for specific knitted products and then decide if you want to make them. The above search results showed searches in the month of September. If you did the same research in December or January, you would see different results.

Let's try another search term like "crochet" and see what shows up:

crochet blanket – 5,798 searches in a month
crochet baby blanket – 3,316 searches
crochet top – 2,927 searches
crochet bag – 2,414 searches
crochet animals – 2,131 searches
crochet socks – 1,928 searches
crochet basket – 1,921 searches

SEO research can reveal product opportunities by showing you how many times per month an item is searched for. However, just because a phrase is highly searched for, it doesn't mean you would necessarily get the same volume of orders. The research simply indicates the demand.

The above is a sampling of what can be learned through SEO keyword research tools. This research is a valuable step in getting your product listings more visitors and buyers.

## Keyword Tools

Etsy provides free "Search Analytics" for sellers with a sales history. This is invaluable if you have been on Etsy for at least a few months and made sales. Etsy shows you which keywords buyers used to find and purchase your product. To view your Etsy analytics, go to your Shop Manager > Marketing > Search analytics. We'll dive more into Etsy in the next chapter.

Other tools to help you research include Etsyrank.com and Marmalead.com; both are subscription services that make keyword research easier for Etsy sellers. Serious Amazon Handmade sellers may want to consider subscribing to MerchantWords.com. Their tool gives search terms used by real buyers on Amazon.

Are these tools expensive? Subscription fees vary. If you can uncover new search terms that result in increased sales, it can be worth the investment, even if you only use the service for one month. You can export your research, save the search data files, and then cancel your subscription. Search terms are seasonal and can change over time, so come back to the tools every few months.

A note about using Google for research: other sellers use Google for competitive research. So if you use an SEO tool that tells you how many searches on Google were made for a particular phrase, know that those searchers aren't all buyers.

Whatever methods you play with for your keyword research, start off with a list of words and phrases you think best describe your items. Then use the keyword tools to find related terms and phrases used by searchers.

Most services let you export your research results as a spreadsheet file, from which you can sort and arrange the results according to your needs.

SEO may seem intimidating, but even a little research can go a long way to uncovering keyword phrases shoppers are using every day to find fashionable products like yours.

Keyword research can also help more people find your blog articles, your posts on Instagram, Pinterest, Facebook, and Twitter, and your product listings on Etsy.

## Inbound Links to Your Pages

Using popular keywords is an important part of SEO for Etsy, Amazon, and other online stores. But there's another element that can affect your ranking in Google, Yahoo, and Bing search results—inbound links pointing to your product listing pages. An example of an inbound link: a blogger writes a review about one of your products and includes a link to your Etsy store.

Inbound links add authority to your page rankings because they are like votes coming in to tell the search engine that your page is relevant for the text in the link.

If you wanted to rank higher for "dangle earrings" in Google searches, you would ask some sites to link to you with the link text reading "dangle earrings." Hidden from the viewer is the actual hyperlink that leads to your page.

But you have to be careful not to go overboard with getting a bunch of inbound links saying the same thing. Google sees this as spam. Instead, you want a variety of inbound link texts. Some inbound link texts could be your URL. Some could be the phrase for which you want to rank high. And others could be semantically-related phrases or your business name.

## Engagement

Another factor that influences your SEO rankings is the amount and frequency of engagement your page receives from real people. For example, you post a video on your Facebook page with a link to your Etsy store. Your followers click through your link and check out your product pages. That engagement, including how much time a visitor spends, is tracked and measured by Google, which then becomes part of the algorithm that determines how Google will rank your pages for keywords.

## Where to Place Keywords and Tags

Placing popular tags in your Etsy, Amazon, and other online shop product listing pages increases your chances of getting found in search. Here are the areas where you can make use of tags in your product listings for SEO purposes:

* **Title:** The first 40 characters (first few words) of your title are the most important for SEO, so include the most popular buyer keywords at the beginning.
* **Description:** Create a product description that promises benefits to the buyer. Insert popular keywords and tags throughout.
* **Attributes:** Attributes are extra tags like colors and materials. People search for "red" scarves or "cotton" clothing.
* **"About" page:** Your artist's story is an often-overlooked area to include your keywords. Weave them into your personal narrative.

**\* Shop announcement:** Yet another area where you can include popular search terms.

**\* Tags:** Use all allowable tags. They should differ from each other. Optimally, tags should match as many of the words in your product's title as possible.

**\* Categories:** Categories act like tags so choose categories relevant to your product line. But if you sell scarves under the category "Scarves" don't waste one of your tags with the word "scarves."

**\* Shop policies and terms:** Include your popular search terms in your policies content. This content does get read by Google and may appear in search results.

One and two-word tags like "mittens" or "hand bag" are too broad for you to rank well for. Multi-word phrases are both easier to rank for and more likely to be used by someone ready to buy.

For example, "tote bag" is a popular search term (over 90,000 searches on Google in a recent month) but not necessarily one used by shoppers alone.

Whereas, "black tote bag" (8,100 searches in the same recent month) is more specific and used by those shopping for exactly that.

Though your primary keywords should be phrases used by buyers, there is an overall SEO benefit to including a mix of both broad and specific search terms in your product descriptions.

### WordPress SEO

For bloggers using WordPress, it may feel like too much trouble to keep up with SEO and provide content. Fortunately, there is an easy-to-use, free plugin called Yoast SEO. Yoast scans your blog posts and suggests how many keywords to use, where to place them, how long your content should be, the readability of your content, and more SEO goodies.

*Seasonal SEO*

With a basic knowledge of SEO, you can take advantage of seasonal searches. For instance, shoppers search for "Christmas gifts for men" or "girlfriend gifts for Valentines" in the weeks and months leading up to those shopping times.

Change your tags on your product listings throughout the year to position your products for those special occasions. Start using seasonal tags at least two months in advance to give search engines like Google time to index your listings.

\* \* \* \* \* \*

## Losing Your Job May Be the Best Thing

*When Reuben Reuel lost his job decided to work for himself. He created his own fashion line, Demestik, using fabrics designed from traditional African styles. Reuel's Etsy store earned him a consistent five-star rating, from over 5,000 sales. His designs have been worn by singer Beyoncé and other celebrities. Source: HuffPost.com*

\* \* \* \* \* \*

Selling on Etsy requires more than throwing up a bunch of product listings and hoping buyers flock to your online shop. The next chapter prepares you for what you need to know to succeed in this major online marketplace for consumers looking to buy handmade.

# CHAPTER 8

# Selling on Etsy

E tsy has over 35 million active buyers browsing handmade products from almost two million sellers. Etsy buyers are loyal—81% are repeat customers who account for annual sales exceeding three billion dollars.

As a selling platform, Etsy makes it easy to get started for new sellers to set up a shop and add product listings. If you aren't already a member, begin by registering for an account. Then click on "Sell on Etsy" to start.

The Etsy Seller Guide at etsy.com/seller-handbook will get you up and running using best practices from successful sellers.

YouTube offers hundreds of free tutorial videos on all aspects of setting up an Etsy store. Many of them will be trailers or lead magnets for paid courses. But you can get a lot of solid tips for free.

The best practices outlined in this chapter will help you set up your Etsy shop to succeed. Here you will learn about:

- Setup steps
- Product listings
- Images
- Etsy SEO
- Your product descriptions
- Share on social media
- How to treat customers
- Etsy ads
- Market your Etsy store offline
- If sales are poor
- Get reviews and publicity
- Blogging

- Etsy apps
- Mailing list

## Setup Steps

* Brand your Etsy shop by naming it with your business name. The name shows up in your Etsy shop URL. Example: https://www.etsy.com/shop/YourBizName. You can shorten this URL for business cards using the free tool https://www.bit.ly/.

* Decide what you will sell and make a list of your products. For ideas, review Chapter 1. Each product will have its own listing.

* Research popular keywords buyers use to find products like yours (EtsyRank.com).

* Write a description for each product.

* Take photos of your items from different angles. Etsy allows you to upload ten images for each product.

* Read and follow all the guidelines and store policies when setting up your shop.

## Shop Info and Appearance

* Add your artist's story to your Seller's Bio. Shoppers want to know about your creative journey.

* Your "Shop Announcement" gives you a place to add interesting details about your products and your creative process. It is also an overlooked area for placing popular keyword phrases used by Etsy shoppers.

* Design and upload a shop icon, profile image of yourself and (optional) store banner.

## Shop Policies

* Write a welcome message. If natural, weave in popular search terms. They won't help you here with Etsy search rankings but will help you get found by Google.

* Create your Payment, Shipping, Refund, Seller, and Additional Information policies. Don't omit these as Etsy search favors shops with completed policies.

# Improve Your Product Listings

* Product listings are pages that display information to viewers about your product. Listings include images, a title, a product description, tags, price, shipping, quantity, and materials.

* When setting up a product listing, fill in each section. Each of the areas on the listing page provides another opportunity to appear in searches.

* Create separate listings for each color of the same item. Each listing is an added entrance to your shop through search. For example, people search for red scarves, black scarves, brown scarves, and more colors. If you make a listing for a red scarf and a separate listing for a black scarf and another listing for a brown scarf, you have tripled your potential landing pages.

* More product listings are better. Go back to Chapter 1 and think about how you might expand into new lines.

* If you have customer reviews, include them in your product listing description. Even though viewers can access your reviews elsewhere, repeating one or more of the best ones in the description adds social proof that your product is worth buying.

## Images

Images play a major role when online shoppers browse your listings. Ninety percent of shoppers report that great photos played a part in their buying decision. Take photos of an item from different angles. Include images of people using your item and images of the product with a plain white background. See Appendix 1 for more on photography.

## Etsy SEO

In the last chapter, you learned the basics of SEO. You saw keyword search terms used by buyers looking for fashion crafts. Here we look at SEO tips specifically to help your Etsy shop listings get found more often in searches.

* The most important areas for SEO of your Etsy listings are titles, tags, and descriptions.

* Popular search terms (gathered from EtsyRank or Marmalead) used in your listing titles, tags, and descriptions can also be worked into other areas of your store like your story, shop policies, and announcements.

* Etsy allows you thirteen keyword tags for each listing. Use all of them. As much as possible, your listing's title should match your tags.

* Include related search terms in your product listing description.

* Shops with a few items in a category rank lower in search compared to shops with many listings in the same category.

* Categories are search terms themselves. Don't waste your tags by including the same keyword as both a category and a tag. For instance, if you create a listing under the category of "tote bags," do not also use one of your thirteen allowable tags for "tote bags."

* Add new item listings to your Etsy store regularly but not all at once. Aim for a minimum of fifty to a hundred listings. Each listing is a new opportunity to be found in Etsy searches, especially if you use unique keywords and tags in each listing.

* Use Etsy's "Search analytics." Access it through Shop Manager > Marketing > Search analytics. It's not so useful for new sellers because there isn't much traffic or sales to analyze. But if you have been on Etsy awhile and made sales, the search analytics tool will tell you which search words shoppers used to find your items converted to sales. Search analytics revealed my shop was getting traffic for search terms I had not used in my tags or listing titles. I went back in and added the terms as tags in a few listings and sales increased.

## Product Descriptions

* In your product descriptions, tell the customer how your item will transform their life. Features are great, but benefits sell. If applicable, how many ways can a person use your item?

* Spell-check your listings before posting. When shoppers see misspelled words or grammatical errors, they may imagine your item is as carelessly assembled as your text.

* Add a shipping profile or select a shipping profile you want to update. Fill out the shipping profile. Select your order processing time (how long it will take to ship your order). The shorter the processing time the more you will convert visitors to customers.

## Share on Social Media

After you have posted your listings, it's time to share. Etsy makes it easy for you to share your product listings, five-star reviews, items that have been recently favorited, and special sales to your social profiles on Pinterest, Facebook, Instagram, and Twitter.

To make use of this feature, go to your Shop Manager > Marketing > Social Media and then look for the tab near the top that reads, "Social accounts." From there, connect your other social profiles. After you have connected your social profiles to Etsy, you are ready to post. Look for and click on the "+Create Post" button. Then Etsy walks you through creating and sharing a post to all your sites. Etsy's tool is free.

If posting frequently is taking too much of your time, schedule your social sharing with tools (subscriptions) like Buffer.com, Hootsuite.com or Tailwindapp.com.

## How to Treat Customers

* When someone messages you through Etsy, respond quickly. It builds goodwill. When I get a message from an Etsy shopper with a question, I respond right away. Customers always thank me for my prompt reply.

* Etsy allows you to program a Thank You message that goes out automatically upon a sale. Express your gratitude for their purchase and tell them when they can expect to get their order.

* Another way to automate building customer relationships is to create a discount coupon for the next purchase. You have the option to set it to go to every customer upon checkout. Go to Shop Manager > Marketing > Sales and Coupons.

* If you get complaints, offer to replace the problem item or issue a refund. Put the customer in control. Don't make them feel they are wrong.

* Just fix problems, even if doing so costs you extra. You've heard the saying, "the customer is always right." It has never been truer than with online sales.

* If you receive a negative review, get in touch with the customer and take care of any issues. After you have made things right, ask the disgruntled shopper to alter their negative rating. Offer a refund or substantial discount coupon if it means getting better feedback.

* Print and include a packing slip that Etsy creates for each order so customers know where the product is coming from. I write on it a big "Thank You" with the person's name at the top.

* Let shoppers know when they can expect their order to ship and make it as soon as you confidently can. Click Shop Manager > Settings > Shipping settings.

## Etsy Ads

A way to potentially boost your Etsy sales is through their "Etsy ads" feature under "Marketing" in your "Shop Manager," but only test ads after you have had sales organically. This is because you want to know that your listing converts visitors to buyers before you put money into ads.

Choose listings you want to promote and set a daily spending budget. Set your initial budget at the minimum so you can affordably test results. After a few weeks, go back in and view your promoted listings statistics.

If you haven't read the chapter on pricing and calculated your profit margins, do it before testing any ads.

Etsy does the keyword analysis for the ads—you don't have to do anything except turn the "Etsy ads" feature on and set a budget. You only pay when someone clicks through from an ad to your product listing.

After you enable ads on Etsy, monitor the results every few days. After about two weeks, look at your sales and your ad spend. Does the profit margin (difference between cost and revenue) justify spending more on ads or indicate you should turn ads off?

## Market Your Etsy Store Offline

Funneling offline shoppers to your Etsy store helps you gather more reviews and build social proof.

Wear or carry something you make whenever you leave the house. When someone comments, hand them your business card—printed with your Etsy store URL—and enthusiastically tell them, "You can see my entire line at my Etsy store!"

Over twenty percent of my Etsy buyers come from my business cards collected by shoppers visiting my craft show booths.

I tell store buyers who see my display at a craft show how they can place an order through my Etsy store using a 50% off coupon.

Home parties and trunk shows are other venues for mentioning your Etsy store.

## If Sales Are Poor

* If your Etsy shop has been up for a while but is performing poorly, hire successful Etsy sellers to critique it. You can get shop reviews on Etsy for anywhere from $20 to $100 or more. Save money at Fiverr.com and search for "etsy review."

* When using Fiverr, only work with providers who have all five-star reviews. I bought three reviews because I wanted different perspectives of my shop. You might think all of them would offer the same suggestions. Though on some points they agreed, each reviewer gave unique ideas that helped my sales.

* Browse the community forums and teams (groups) on Etsy to learn and share experiences with other craft artists about setting up, marketing, and running an Etsy store.

* List more items. Increasing the number of your product listings can boost your sales. You'll have more pages through which shoppers can find you. And Etsy search appears to favor shops that have more items than other sellers in the same category.

* Run discount coupons for key shopping dates. Etsy provides you with a calendar of peak buying seasons with tips for tying in special offers. Go to Shop Manager > Marketing > Key shopping dates.

* Boost sales by offering free shipping, if your profit margin allows it. Etsy created a seller option called Guaranteed Free Shipping for orders over $35. Sellers who opt in to the program get priority in search results over sellers who do not offer free shipping. You can also go into your Shop Manager > Marketing > Sales and coupons. By using Etsy's free shipping coupon (choose "no end date"), Etsy displays a free shipping badge on your shop's product pages. If you set up free shipping as a shipping option, you won't get the Etsy badge. The Etsy badge helps your listings show up better in search results. Even if you have to raise your prices to cover shipping, it will increase your visits and sales.

\* \* \* \* \* \*

## Etsy and Beyond

*You will hear and read many complaints of how Etsy doesn't work for sellers, but you won't hear successful sellers whining. Those who work hard at mastering the Etsy platform get enviable results.*

*In 2015, Alicia Shaffer's Etsy shop, Three Bird Nest, reportedly earned around $1 million from her bohemian-styled accessories and apparel. She credits her success to putting attention on her product photography.*

*ThreeBirdNest.com is now home to her boho product line where visitors see every product photographed in a lifestyle setting and often as part of an ensemble.*

\* \* \* \* \* \*

## Get Reviews and Publicity

Shopping blogs and social media influencers seek new products to review. But the competition for getting reviews can be tough. Magazines, newspapers, and freelance writers also report on handmade fashion products they think will interest their readers. See Chapter 13 for more about getting free publicity from influencers.

Etsy is great for learning how to set up and promote an e-commerce site for your handmade needle crafts. After you master Etsy selling, test other platforms or start your own website. The next chapter introduces more ways to sell online, including Handmade on Amazon.

# CHAPTER 9

# E-commerce Alternatives to Etsy

Though Etsy may be the most popular market for handmade products, there are other options to help you grow your sales and broaden your online presence.

Amazon Handmade is a category on Amazon available to their 300 million+ shoppers. Sites like Artfire, Zibbet, and others also compete with Etsy to attract shoppers looking to buy handmade. Another option is setting up your own website.

With so many possibilities, you may feel you have to choose between them. But there is no rule that says you can only sell in one marketplace. Test them and measure the results. Then focus on any and all platforms that bring you sales and healthy profit margins.

In this chapter, you will learn about:
- Selling on Amazon Handmade
- Alternatives to Etsy and Amazon
- Getting a domain-name website
- Blogging

## Selling on Amazon Handmade

Amazon Handmade opened in 2015. Reviews by maker-sellers have been mixed. Those who have done well report better sales than Etsy. My own Amazon Handmade sales are twice that of my Etsy sales, though my profit margin is much lower per sale because of Amazon's higher seller fees.

Applying and getting set up as a seller on Amazon Handmade is more complex than other online marketplaces for handmade products. The application link is: https://services.amazon.com/handmade/handmade.html.

If accepted, you must subscribe to their Professional Account for sellers. The monthly charge of around $40 was being waived for Handmade sellers as an incentive, but that could change by the time you read this book.

On the plus side, Amazon has a huge marketplace of buyers. Sellers get access to Seller Central, a back office with in-depth analytics and reports on how often your item was viewed, clicked on, and sold.

*What to know about selling on Amazon Handmade:*

* Seller fees are fifteen percent of the retail price. This is higher than Etsy's five percent. Calculate your profit margins before you sign up.

* Setting up product page listings is straightforward. You can copy and paste your Etsy listings content.

* Your products may sell great on Amazon but do poorly on Etsy and vice versa. Test product listings on both sites over a month's time to learn what sells where.

* Amazon Handmade gives you an Artisan's Profile, where you can paste in your artist's story and upload images of yourself.

* Amazon allows sellers to promote their handmade products through Sponsored Product ads. You can access reports that reveal which keyword searches result in sales. You can also learn how the cost of your ads compares to your sales. This lets you adjust your ads to run only those that result in a healthy profit margin.

* If your profit margin allows, consider FBA (Fulfilled By Amazon). Through this program, you ship (at your expense) your products to Amazon warehouses. They fulfill orders to their more than ninety million Amazon Prime member buyers. Amazon Prime members get free shipping and buy more often than non-members.

* An alternative way to tap into Amazon Prime buyers is to use Seller-Fulfilled Prime. Under this program, your buyers get free shipping (because you agree to pay it) but you do the packing and shipping instead of sending products to Amazon FBA warehouses.

\* With 85% of Amazon shoppers reporting they hesitate to make a purchase because of shipping charges, offering free shipping sets you apart from most sellers.

\* If you don't use FBA or Seller Fulfilled Prime, you must set up shipping settings.

\* As with all e-commerce sites, SEO plays a big role in getting views and sales from a site's marketplace. Go to the Amazon Handmade category and start typing in words that describe your product. Amazon will start to auto-populate your search with suggested keywords. Those suggested words come from searches that have resulted in sales.

\* Place the most popular keywords at the beginning of your title and your product descriptions. Amazon allows for additional keywords—similar to Etsy tags—in each listing.

\* Consider using a service like MerchantWords.com to discover buyer search terms. Starting from your own list of words and phrases, MerchantWords delivers a list of keywords you may not have thought of. You'll also see how strong the competition is for your products.

\* Make customer service your top priority. Amazon shoppers weigh other buyer reviews before making purchases. Double-check your product and packaging quality before shipping. Be willing to refund an unhappy customer.

\* \* \* \* \* \*

## Got a Wild Idea to Fix a Common Problem?

*Sara started to dress for a party. Uh oh, her pantyhose didn't look right under her pants. Necessity and invention, right? She cut the feet off her control-top pantyhose, giving birth to a new underwear line. That's how SPANX was born: solving nuisances waiting in our closets and drawers. Sara Blakely's SPANX brand has ballooned into multiple product lines. Her brand and popularity earned her tons of mentions in the media. By 2012, Forbes magazine had named her the world's youngest self-made female billionaire.*

\* \* \* \* \* \*

## Alternatives to Etsy and Amazon

Though Etsy and Amazon Handmade have the largest buyer marketplaces for handmade products, there are other sites worth checking out. The top Etsy and Amazon Handmade alternatives in the US:

- Artfire.com
- BigCartel.com
- Zibbet.com
- IndieMade.com
- iCraftGifts.com
- eCrater.com
- Bonanza.com

See Appendix 3 for places to sell online around the world.

Some seller sites charge a small percentage when a sale is made. Some charge a monthly or yearly fee and allow you to upload as many listings as you want. Each site has a different set of terms, so read the fine print to avoid surprises.

## Setting Up Your Own Domain Site

Many sellers prefer having a domain-name website. With your own site, you are independent of whatever changes a large outfit like Etsy or Amazon makes.

One of the big complaints about Etsy, Amazon, and the other online shop providers is that they own the customers, not you. Setting up your own domain site lets you blog, capture e-mails, provide a customer newsletter, offer specials, announce new products, and otherwise operate like other e-commerce sites.

Building a site from scratch can be stressful and time-consuming. Using services and tools like Wix or WordPress allows you to set up a basic site in less than an hour.

*Steps for DIY setting up a domain site:*

- Your business name is the best choice for your domain name as it helps you brand your business. If you can't get the exact name, try adding a short word before or after your domain name and check for availability again.

- Once you settle on your name, register it at a site like NameCheap.com or GoDaddy.com. The annual fee to keep your domain name is anywhere from $9 to $20, depending on the registrar.
- After you have registered your domain name, you need a web host. Some registrars also provide hosting. If not, there are thousands to choose from. HostGator.com and BlueHost.com have received good reviews.
- All web hosts walk you through connecting your domain name to their servers so that your website will be visible online.
- The next step is creating and uploading pages with content. Sellers usually include: home page, about the artist page, shopping page, contact page, subscribe page and a blog page if you plan to blog.
- WordPress, a free web-building application available from most web hosts, provides everything you need. It offers free themes, free e-commerce plugins and lots of free support. WordPress sites are popular for e-commerce and for blogging.
- If you aren't using WordPress with a shopping-cart plugin, you will need to build an online catalog and process transactions. Shopify and BigCommerce are two of the most popular shopping-cart programs.

## Online Advertising

Ad campaigns or promoted listings have paid off for some sellers but not all. You can only know if they work for your products by testing.

When testing ads, limit your risk by setting a low daily budget for ad spending and an end date for a campaign.

If you get sales organically, it means your product page is likely to convert shoppers who come through ads. Therefore, scaling up your sales through advertising makes sense.

But the reverse is also true. If your product page doesn't already produce sales, throwing money into ads could be wasteful.

As I have mentioned several times, know your profit margins if you intend to grow your business. Ads are one way to boost your sales, but there's no guarantee they will.

Before you start a campaign, determine how much you can afford and are willing to lose and then test ads. If your test ad campaign loses money, stop running the ads; if your test makes enough money that you still earn a profit from each sale, increase your ad spend / daily budget gradually, continuing to measure results.

### *Checklist for Running Ads*

Ad options differ from site to site. Sometimes they are called "Promoted Listings."
- Test ad campaigns with a small daily budget.
- Run ads long enough to get 2,000 impressions.
- Measure click-throughs and cost of sales.
- If you have the budget, test different audiences.
- Drop ads that don't result in sales.
- Gradually increase ad campaigns that convert at low cost of sales, continuing to monitor spending vs. profit.

Another way to earn income is through self-publishing patterns, books, and other forms of content. The next chapter explores ways to generate ongoing revenue turning your crafting skills into digital products.

# CHAPTER 10

# Make Money Publishing Patterns, Books, and More

T his chapter teaches you how to earn income from your knitting, crochet, needlecraft, and other crafting skills by publishing patterns, books, e-books, audio books, magazines, newsletters, and more.

Publishing has the potential to give you additional part-time or possibly full-time income streams. Create your patterns or books once and sell them thousands of times.

I have met many craft artists who, like me, were also authors. I wrote and self-published my first book based on my experiences as a fiber craft artist in 1991. One thing led to another and I found myself with a string of self-published books and offers to speak and teach for money.

Another reason to consider publishing: there may come a day when you can no longer physically work on your craft as often as you once did. Books and patterns you have written can add financial support over many years. A book I first published in 1995 continues to earn me a small income all these years later. Of course, not all books and patterns will sell forever, but some can remain steady sellers for years.

Here you will learn about:
- Types of content in demand that you can publish and sell.
- Publishing patterns.
- Where to sell your patterns.
- Software or services needed to start publishing.

# Types of Content in Demand to Publish and Sell

Books are not the only form of content you can self-publish and capitalize on. Here are other digital products and services you can develop from your crafting skills and experiences:

**Patterns:** There is a consistent demand for patterns from quilters, needleworkers, knitters, doll makers, sewing enthusiasts, and more. The top three Etsy stores selling downloadable patterns have combined sales of around 460,00 at the time of this writing. Prices for a pattern for a single project average $5 to $7.

Below are search statistics for patterns on Etsy and on Amazon:

*Etsy searches:*
- mask patterns – 18,105 monthly searches (temporarily popular due to Covid)
- crochet patterns – 11,553 monthly searches
- sewing patterns – 5,827 monthly searches
- quilt patterns – 4,275 monthly searches
- knitting patterns – 2,219 monthly searches
- doll patterns – 2,057 monthly searches

*Amazon searches:*
- masks pattern – 1,800 monthly searches
- crochet patterns – 14,700 monthly searches
- sewing patterns – 29.000 monthly searches
- quilt patterns – 7,400 monthly searches
- knitting patterns – 4,400 monthly searches
- doll patterns – 2,700 monthly searches

**Printables:** Though it's a competitive category, Etsy sellers are selling their downloadable designs under a category called "Printables" at https://www.etsy.com/market/printables. For example, take one of your fiber craft images. Overlay a quote. Save it as a downloadable PDF. Sell on Etsy.

**Gift cards:** A couple traveling across the US supported themselves selling her poetry and his art on self-published gift cards and posters. Their business, Blue Mountain Arts, eventually grew into a global company worth hundreds of millions.

**Calendars:** We need calendars every year. Get great photos of your best pieces and publish eye-catching calendars to sell at gift stores, yarn shops, and online at Amazon.

**Newsletters:** Hobbyists are hungry for tips, hacks, and resources for making more cute stuff. Newsletters can be printed and mailed or e-mailed via autoresponders. Building a list of subscribers provides you a steady monthly income.

**Mini-books:** Mini-books are condensed versions of larger books. Mini-books are typically smaller in size and can easily fit in a purse or handbag. They make great gifts.

**E-books** (Kindle, Epub, PDF): Sell your content as e-book digital downloads. You have no upfront costs or inventory to manage. See *KDP Publishing Fast Track* for the system I follow for self-publishing e-books.

**Audio books:** Often overlooked by authors is the growing market for audio books. Because there is little competition in this area, authors can easily dominate their niche by creating audio editions of their content.

**Special reports:** If you have specialized knowledge about a craft technique, tool or equipment pattern or anything not quite enough to make a book, create a special report. They are often perceived as higher value than books because of their specialized and difficult to find topics.

**Mobile apps:** Got an idea to make a craft project go smoother? Consider creating a mobile app. It's not as difficult as it seems. Mobile app templates make it as simple as plug in your content and publish. You can charge for the app or make it free but users must see your ads. When they click on the ads, you earn per click. Google "mobile app templates" for sources. Code Canyon (https://codecanyon.net/category/mobile) offers hundreds of templates.

\* \* \* \* \* \*

## How One Couple Is Making $600,000 a Year Selling Digital Goods

*Jason and Cinnamon Miles started selling their patterns. In 2013 they launched Pixie Faire in the sewing niche. It is now the Internet's largest doll clothes pattern marketplace with over 100 designers and over 3.3 million patterns downloaded.*

*Pixie Faire has been featured by Shopify as a case studies on their blog. The article, "How One Couple Is Making $600,000 A Year Selling Digital Goods" has been a reader favorite for many years. See: https://www.shopify.com/blog/17587420-how-one-couple-is-making-600-000-per-year-selling-digital-products*

\* \* \* \* \* \*

## Publishing Patterns

Do digital patterns sell on Etsy? According to Craftcount.com, one of the top Etsy selling shops is Thevelvetacorn with more than 300,000 sales of crochet patterns.

If you are detail-oriented, pattern publishing may be your ticket to extra money. Of course, you must have gone through the steps from your original and unique design to finished product yourself. Write out the steps as if you were teaching someone else.

The clearer you can describe each phase in the creation process, the better your final patterns will be received and reviewed.

*Here are the steps to creating and publishing your patterns:*

**1. Name your pattern.** You may not have a cute name when you start, but make a list of prospective titles and narrow it down to one you love.

**2. Make a supply list.** List material, thread, accessories or anything else that goes into the project.

**3. Clearly and in short simple language, write out each step** in the process clearly. Include all measurements needed to complete each step.

**4. Take photos** or draw illustrations of each step.

**5. Edit your text** for spelling, grammar and typos. Hire a proofreader, too, because your own eyes can pass over a common error someone else catches immediately.

**6. Improve your images** in Photoshop or similar program. Whether you are using drawings, illustrations, or photos, they need to be converted to the proper resolution. To assure you get a sharp looking publication, images should be set at 300 dpi, .TIF format and CMYK mode. If you are using a graphic designer for this part of the project, don't stress, they will know what those settings mean.

**7. Decide on the ultimate trim size** of your completed pattern. Will it be 6" x 9", 8.5" x 11" or something else? You need the trim size established before you can set up documents in the layout application you use to format the interior pages.

**8. Design your cover**. Browse the best selling patterns similar to yours for cover concepts. Use an image of the completed project and place text over the image. Designing the cover is not only fun, but it can motivate you to complete the rest of the project.

**9. Format and layout the interior** text with images placed appropriately prior to publication. See the following section for software apps for layout and design. As a side note, don't let learning software hold you back. YouTube has tutorial videos on almost every software needed to format books and patterns.

**10. Save or export the document as a PDF**. PDFs can be downloaded from a web site or they can be used by a printer to produce hard copy editions of your pattern. Check with your printer prior to submitting the PDF file to them because they will give you the correct PDF output settings for their equipment.

**11. Before you publish, test your pattern**. Send your completed pattern to friends who make similar items. Ask them if your steps are clear, if the images tell the story and the supply list is accurate.

**12. Price your pattern** in line with similar published patterns in your media. It's what people are used to paying.

**13. Publish** / upload your completed pattern to one or more of the sites below:

## Where to Sell Your Patterns

- https://www.etsy.com/seller-handbook/article/how-to-sell-digital-downloads-on-etsy/47330319230
- https://www.ravelry.com/wiki/pages/DesignerQuick-StartGuide
- https://www.spoonflower.com/
- https://creativemarket.com/
- https://help.bigcartel.com/pulley
- https://www.zazzle.com/sell
- https://www.deramores.com/pages/designer-submissions
- https://designers.lovecrafts.com/
- http://www.kollabora.com/faq-vendors
- http://www.e-junkie.com/
- https://gumroad.com/
- https://www.printmepretty.co.uk/ (UK)

Distributors for reaching stores:
- https://my.modafabrics.com/about-us/catalogs
- https://www.checkerdist.com/category/books

## Software and Services to Start Publishing

After you have a clear idea or concept of what to publish, you will need software or applications to format and transform your raw content into attractive looking documents that can be uploaded to a printer and/or downloaded to buyers.

Here are some paid and free resources for creating your content.

**Canva**: https://www.canva.com/ provides templates for creating books, e-books, book covers, gift cards, posters, banners, and more. Basic membership is free.

**Scrivener**: https://www.literatureandlatte.com/scrivener/overview Scrivener is a very popular writing software that helps authors organize and format their content.

**OpenOffice**: http://www.openoffice.org/ is a free, open source alternative to Microsoft Office. It includes a writing /

word processing module, a spreadsheet, a presentation maker and more.

**InDesign**: https://www.adobe.com/creativecloud.html InDesign is used by book and publication designers to layout and prepare content suitable for printing. By itself, the program is pricey at several hundred dollars. Subscribing to Adobe Creative Cloud makes it more affordable per monthly rate according to how many of their applications you use.

**Affinity Publisher**: https://affinity.serif.com/en-gb/publisher/ is an open source (free) alternative to InDesign.

**Photoshop**: https://adobe.com/creativecloud.html Photoshop, also from Adobe, is a popular image and graphic design tool. As with InDesign, it's expensive when bought by itself, but cheaper at as a monthly subscription.

**Gimp**: https://www.gimp.org/ is a free open source alternative to Photoshop.

The above applications require a learning curve if you aren't already familiar with them. Fortunately, there are numerous free tutorial videos available for each on YouTube.

If you don't want to do your own layout and design, you can outsource it. I have often used providers at fiverr.com and upwork.com who will quote layout and design work according to the size of your project. When browsing for services, look for providers who have done lots of jobs and have positive reviews.

After your content has been formatted, you are ready to print or upload a digital file. For digital products, each site you plan to sell from may have slightly different procedures but follow their instructions for uploading, describing and pricing your product.

For example, on Etsy, you create a product listing for a digital product similar to a physical product, but you will be prompted to upload your file. When customers pay, they are sent a download link.

For digital e-books, there is Kindle Direct Publishing by Amazon at https://kdp.amazon.com/en_US/ and a number of alternative distributors like Smashwords at https://www.smashwords.com and Draft2Digital at https://draft2digital.com/.

Smashwords and Draft2Digital distribute e-books to resellers that Amazon doesn't reach.

For print-on-demand books, https://kdp.amazon.com/en_US/ lets you upload your files and turn them into printed books. After your file has been approved, they send you a proof copy. When you approve the proof, your book will be available on Amazon within a day.

Ingram Spark is another option to consider for creating print-on-demand books; owned by Ingram Books (https://www.ingramspark.com/), largest wholesaler of books in the world. There is a set up fee per book, but once in their system, your book is available on-demand through their global database.

Just ahead, another way to market online is by publishing interesting content through blogging, which is mostly free except for the time you invest. For some sellers, blogging has paid off with increased sales and a larger mailing list of followers.

# CHAPTER 11

# Blogging

Adding a blog to your marketing mix allows you to publish articles, images and videos around topics related to your knitted, crocheted, or other needlecrafted products and grow your e-mail mailing list. Because search engines love new content, blog pages often rank higher in Google search results than static web pages.

Blogging is a way to express yourself without editing, an instant way to get published, a journal from which to sprout product news, and a way to create a community.

It's also a way to attract and stay in touch with new customers. People who read your blog get to know you as a human being rather than a marketer. Eighty-one percent of U.S. online consumers rely on advice from blogs according to Blogher.com.

Each blog post is a new web page. The more pages you have, the more opportunities Google can show you in search results.

You can create free blogs on WordPress.org, Blogger.com, Medium.com and many other places. Or you can buy a domain name, get it hosted and publish a blog from the site using WordPress as a platform.

WordPress is the most popular and the easiest blogging platform. Go on YouTube and search for "wordpress tutorial" to find hundreds of free videos that walk you through the process step by step.

\* \* \* \* \* \*

## Knitting Blogger

*NobleKnits has grown into one of the top knitting blogs with over 300,000 visitors a month.*

*Nancy Queen, a knitting and crochet expert, provides knitting and crochet tips, inspiration, and tutorials. Nancy is author of four books on needle crafting, has owned two yarn stores, appeared on QVC with how-to kits, and helped thousands of crafters.*

\* \* \* \* \* \*

## Tips for Blogging Success

\* Articles with images and videos of your handmade products get almost 100% more views, so make your posts media-rich.

\* Post useful content like how-to articles, related products to yours in the news, consumer trends, and other resources.

\* For every seven to ten useful content posts, write a post that pitches one of your products like a new product, sale, or event where you'll be displaying.

\* WordPress plugins, Zapier.com and IFTTT.com let you automatically syndicate posts and images from your blogs to multiple social media sites.

\* WordPress plugins like Etsy Shop (free) let you connect and display your Etsy shop listings so you don't have to use a separate shopping cart to process transactions.

\* After your blog is up and running, see Chapter 13 about getting free publicity, including approaching bloggers who review handmade products.

\* Use EtsyRank.com to research popular search words and phrases that Etsy shoppers use every day to find products like yours. Place those words and phrases in your blog article's title, URL, content, image file names, and tags.

As a blogger, you can take advantage of social media to get fresh eyes on your content for free. But promoting through social media takes finesse and time. Keep reading to discover best practices used by indie makers and designers to grow their social following.

# CHAPTER 12

# Promote on Social Media

Social media offers multiple ways to grow a fan base for your handmade needlecrafted products. Social sites attract different types of audiences according to their preferences. For instance, Facebook fans respond to or engage with posts in one way, fans on Instagram another.

Rather than attempt to master marketing on all social sites, go for getting results on one or two of the sites you are at ease with before promoting on others.

Handmade sellers spend time on social networking sites to gather new leads, increase sales, and follow up with customers. Sellers can:

1. Post product images and videos
2. Learn what customers think and how they communicate
3. Interact with customers to build relationships
4. Grow their following
5. Link more visitors to an Etsy shop or website
6. Check out what competitors are doing to market their things
7. Create, test and measure ads

To help you start including social media marketing in your handmade business, this chapter covers:

- Social marketing tips
- Scheduling tools
- Move social followers to your e-mail list
- Facebook tips
- Pinterest tips
- Instagram tips
- Twitter tips

# Social Marketing Tips

Before we go into the four main social platforms, the following checklist acts as a primer for social posting:

* Get familiar with how a platform functions. People hang out on social sites for specific reasons. If you learn something that works to promote your Instagram posts, the same tactic may not work on Pinterest or Twitter.

* Focus on learning a social site you like and feel most at ease with.

* Don't expect big returns. Studies show that only 1% to 2% of social site referrals buy on their first visit to a site.

* Some sellers say Instagram sends them more customers. For others, it's Pinterest or Facebook. Which is best for you? Test some posts and measure your results.

* Brief posts with fewer than seventy characters get more interaction than longer posts.

* Post several times a day. Use tools described later in this chapter to schedule post deliverance across sites.

* In your posts, be helpful. Be inspiring. Be entertaining. Be educational.

* Posts with images get more shares on Facebook and the most retweets on Twitter.

* Posts with videos get the most engagement.

* The organic reach of your posts is becoming more limited. To get more viewers, you will have to pay for ads.

* Reply to people's comments on your posts. The more engagement you can get going the more your posts will show up organically.

* How often should you promote your product when posting socially? Start out with seven posts that help, entertain or educate, and then post your product-related article or link. Repeat a few times and notice how your followers respond.

## Social Posts Scheduling Tools

Managing all of your profiles across several sites one at a time can quickly take up your day. In Chapter 8, Selling on

Etsy, one of the tools in your Etsy Shop Manager under Marketing is the Social Media option. You can quickly connect and promote posts of your listings, reviews and favorites directly to your Facebook, Instagram, Pinterest, and Twitter profiles.

There are other scheduling tools (paid subscriptions) to help leverage your time. Try one or more for a month (some offer free trials) and then decide if you want to stay with that tool or try a different one.

- Outfy.com
- Hootsuite.com
- Buffer.com
- Tailwindapp.com
- SproutSocial.com

## Move Social Followers Your Mailing List

If your favorite social site folds or changes policies, or if your account gets shut down, all of your followers and the work you did to get them vanishes. There is no back-up.

You may not own your social followers, but you do own your mailing list. And that list will be yours to promote through regardless of what happens to your social platforms.

To get your followers to give you their e-mail addresses, offer an incentive like a coupon, free download, a newsletter subscription, or a mini course.

Your e-mail list is an asset. Back it up frequently. Use it to stay in touch with your tribe. See Chapter 15 for tips on capturing and making use of your mailing list.

## Facebook Tips

Over two billion people use Facebook. Almost eighty percent of shoppers in the US have found products to buy while on Facebook. Once you have a personal profile set up on Facebook, you can set up a free Facebook page for your business. Facebook personal profiles are limited to adding 5,000 friends, but Facebook pages can have an unlimited number of likes and followers.

\* \* \* \* \* \*

## Fashion and Style Are Popular on Facebook

*Facebook may be the social platform to launch your handmade product line. It's certainly been good for well-known brands. JustFab (https://www. facebook.com/justfab) has over 10 million likes and DressLily (https://www.facebook.com/Dresslily) has more than 11 million fans. RoseGal, started by a group of friends who love vintage, has attracted more than 13 million likes (https://www.facebook. com/rosegalfans).*

\* \* \* \* \* \*

### *Selling from a Facebook Page*

* FB pages let you add content about your products and sell them from the page. You also have access to "Insights" providing visitor data you can't get from a profile page. You will learn how many people your posts reached, how many new likes you got, how many people engaged with your posts, and more.

* Sell directly from your Facebook page by enabling a Facebook Shop tab in your page settings. Shoppers can browse your items, make a purchase, and pay for it while remaining on your Facebook page.

* Getting sales from Facebook means getting visual, big time. Studies show Facebook users respond more to imagery and video than simple text.

* Alternatively, the Shop tab can link to your other website or your Etsy shop. But sending customers away from Facebook creates an added step they have to take and will lower conversion rates.

* To collect payments, set up an account with a payment gateway like Stripe.com. After your payment account is open, add products in your store.

* For a detailed video on setting up a Facebook Shop, see http://bit.ly/setupfacebookstore.

## Posting Tips

* Post consistently, like several times a week.

* Post from your FB Page, not your personal profile.

* Upload images of your products, videos of your creative process and posts with a mix of video, imagery, and text.

* Video content is queen on Facebook. Thirty percent of mobile FB users report that video is their favorite way to find new products.

* Facebook Live videos get six times as many interactions as regular videos. FB Live videos also rank higher in newsfeeds.

* Post useful tips related to your products. If you make accessories, offer tips like "5 ways to use this ____ to look great when you're in a hurry."

* Avoid making politically or religiously charged posts.

## Facebook Stories

When you post to your FB page in the normal way, that post shows up in some but not all of your viewers' feeds. As a person's feed fills up with incoming posts, your message cycles down in the newsfeed as newer posts appear at the top.

FB stories appear above your users' feed and remain there for 24 hours. If you add to your story several times a day, it keeps your business name in front of your fans instead of it vanishing in the feed.

You can add stories to your FB page from your smartphone. They can include photos, videos, and text.

Stories work best as a "behind the scenes" look into your crafts business. For example, you might shoot a video of you knitting a new piece. Or, for fun, completely messing one up.

## "Buy Sell" Groups on Facebook

* FB "Buy Sell" groups for handmade products allow you to post images, product descriptions, and links to your item's sales page on Etsy or elsewhere. Buyers join these groups to browse for handmade items. See Facebook.com/groups/craftsu.

* To find groups on FB to post your products in, type "buy

sell handmade" or "buy sell crafts" in the search bar at the upper left of any FB page. Then click on the Groups tab to narrow results to only look at Groups.

    * Facebook.com/marketplace/ is FB's own buy/sell market. It's used by 800 million people globally each month. Sellers list items for sale. Shoppers browse for bargains. Like with Craigslist, there is no fee to use the marketplace.

    * FB Marketplace displays tons of stuff people are looking to get rid of at low prices. Search results are tailored to your local area.

    * A search for "handmade" brought up hundreds of items near me. Most of the listings were pre-owned items. Some were new and priced at the same retail price the seller asks on Etsy.

    * Though listing handmade products next to used stuff won't set your products apart, your item on FB Marketplace gives you a virtual shopping cart for free. You link directly to your product listing, buyers can pay through Facebook Payments, and you ship the item or deliver it locally.

## Pinterest Tips

Pinterest.com is a visual search engine where you pin your favorite images and videos from across the web. Pins on Pinterest don't expire, so investing time here can pay off in the long term.

The site gets over two billion searches each month. It's considered by many to be the most popular visual search platform. More relevant to sellers, 93% of pinners use Pinterest for planning purchases. The average sale arising from a Pinterest search is close to $60—higher than average sales from Twitter or Facebook buyers.

Fans of Pinterest search for fashion tips, what's in style, plan weddings, baby arrivals, DIY how-tos, and much more. Fashion and DIY are among the top interests on Pinterest.

\*   \*   \*   \*   \*   \*

## Pinterest Loves Etsy

*Not everyone who views your pins or follows you on Pinterest will click through to your online store, but enough do to justify investing time building a presence there. Pins don't disappear like Facebook posts. Even when I have neglected pinning for long periods, my Etsy store statistics show visitors checking out my items from Pinterest almost every day. One of my pins from 2012 still sends traffic to my site.*

\*   \*   \*   \*   \*   \*

### *Setting Up Your Pinterest Profile*

\* Choose the Pinterest business account option when registering. It offers more options including access to Pinterest Analytics, which tracks and measures how engaging your pins are.

\* If you already have a personal profile, convert it to a business account for free.

\* When setting up your profile, choose the same business name you use across all of your online sites.

\* As with every place you sell online, include popular tags/ keywords related to your business in your profile description and when naming your boards so you get discovered in searches.

\* Go to "Settings" and "Claim." Add your website if you have one. Also, claim your Etsy store, Instagram and YouTube accounts. Claiming your accounts gives you access to Analytics that show how visitors engage with your pins.

### *Creating Pinterest Boards*

\* Pinterest boards let you organize your images by topics. After you have set up your profile, your next step is to create five to ten boards to place your pins in.

\* Collect a mix of content browsers will enjoy looking through. For example, if you knit or crochet scarves from sustainable materials, create one board for pins of your scarves, another board with pins teaching people different ways to wear scarves, and another board that shows your scarves worn on special occasions.

* If you don't have a lot of product images of your own to fill in your boards in the beginning, fill them with images of related tips, guides, and products you like.

* Choose a popular keyword tag for the board name. Include a description using several related keywords. Upload an eye-catching cover image. Just as people judge a book by its cover, they explore your pins based on your boards' cover images.

* For examples of how to build out your boards, search Pinterest using words that describe your products or customers; make a list of the most popular pinners and observe how they've created their boards and pins.

### *Gathering Followers*

* Search for topics related to your products and find the most popular boards. When you find someone with a million or more followers, click the "Followers" link on their profile. A drop-down list appears. Start following the popular pinners' followers that appear to be active on Pinterest.

* Follow up to fifty new people every day. If you have set up your boards with interesting image collections, you will find popular pinners' followers following you. Pin new images daily as they show up in your new followers' feeds.

* Engage with your followers. Comment on their pins. Create conversations.

* Join Tailwind Tribes. Here you can join groups (tribes) of like-minded people. You share their posts and they share yours. See: https://www.tailwindapp.com/tribes.

### *Pinning*

* Most Pinterest users are female—think of pins that will appeal to women.

* Pin consistently, even daily. Use a scheduling tool to make this easy.

* Pin images and videos. Pin helpful tips.

* Pinterest favors pins/pinners that get higher engagement with higher search results.

* Pinterest studies reveal that lifestyle images get more attention than product images, 150% more purchases than product photos alone.

* Videos pinned on Pinterest get higher engagement than other sites.

* Optimize pins to get more viewers from search. Each pin can have a description. In the description use popular search terms and tags related to your products. Link directly to your product's listing on Etsy or elsewhere so viewers can click to buy instantly.

* Pin your Etsy listings, five-star reviews, and more on Pinterest through your Etsy Shop Manager.

* Rich pins are a special format that gives more context around an idea or product by displaying extra information on the pin. Rich pins are free, but your pins have to meet requirements and be approved. The steps for setting up rich pins are found at: help.pinterest.com/en/business/article/rich-pins.

### Selling from Pinterest

When pinning your product images, you can link directly to your item's Etsy or other product listing page.

You can also use an app like Shopify to link a pin to a page on your website's shopping cart.

After you have set up a Pinterest business account and claimed your website, you can set up shopping Pins and catalogs. You can feature up to eight product groups.

Product Pins contain metadata and are formatted to let viewers know that they're shoppable. They contain pricing info, availability, product title and description.

For detailed step-by-step help with setting up products for sale on Pinterest, see https://help.pinterest.com/en/business/article/create-a-shop

With a business account on Pinterest, you can access paid advertising through Promoted Pins. As with all ad campaigns, set your spending budget at the minimum dollar amounts, and test for two to three weeks. Pinterest provides ad tracking that reveals how many people view your ads and click through.

## Instagram Tips

Instagram is the app to use to launch your indie fashion brand. It is a mobile-dominated platform for telling visual stories—98% of Instagram content comes from phones.

While Instagram has over a billion users, 59% are under thirty years old. Many Etsy sellers report they get more sales via Instagram than Pinterest or Facebook. Understandable, since over 1,926,000 Instagram users follow Etsy's profile there.

Instagram members have a high engagement rate. Over 70% of users have bought something found there using their mobile phone.

\* \* \* \* \* \*

### Casual and Earth-Friendly

*Michael Natenshon started Marine Layer after his girlfriend threw out his favorite T-shirt. He developed an Earth-friendly fabric made from recycled beech wood. His clothing lines include T-shirts, hoodies, skirts, and fashion for kids. Marine Layer has become a global brand being casual, sustainable, and eco-friendly. See their Instagram account at: instagram.com/marinelayer/.*

\* \* \* \* \* \*

### Set Up an Instagram Account

\* Download the Instagram app and install on your phone. If you plan to use Instagram to promote your handmade items, set up your new account as a business account or convert your existing profile to a business one.

\* Like with other social sites, a business account allows you to promote or advertise your posts. You also get access to

"Insights" (analytics) about your posts, hashtags, visitors, and engagements.

    * Choose the same username (or a close variant if taken) that you use on Etsy and all your social media profiles. Upload the same profile image you use on other social sites.

    * Include a link to your Etsy or other online shop in your profile.

### Posting Images

    * With the app open, take a photo with your phone, write a cute caption, and push "share." You have the option to add image-editing filters before you share your photos.

    * The app automatically sizes your uploaded image to display on mobile devices. Horizontal (portrait) oriented images fit the screen well as most people naturally hold their phones horizontally.

    * Sharing images comes with options. You can share to your other social media profiles. You can add hashtags. You can tag other people in the image. And you can add your location so viewers will know where the image was taken.

    * You can also upload images from your computer.

    * In your post you can add a brief caption. Caption text is found through search, so include relevant hashtags.

### Videos

    * Instagram lets you add and edit videos up to sixty seconds long. Videos can come directly from your phone or from content you have transferred to your phone from another source.

    * Sellers can add a call to action at the end of a video. Just add a line of text in the final moments.

### Instagram Stories

    * Instagram stories, like FB stories, feature your photos and videos at the top of your follower's feeds. They remain there for twenty-four hours.

    * Upload your story-behind-the-scenes of your handmade gig. Post stories about how you got started in your fashion crafts

business, how you make your products, and what inspires you.

* Use the "poll" feature to ask your followers questions. Discover what they think about your stories.

### Hashtags

* Hashtags are mashed-up phrases preceded by the # sign. Example: #handmadewedding. The # sign turns the phrase into a clickable link. Hashtags help your posts get found in search.

* Hashtags can help you uncover other sellers with products like yours.

* Multi-worded hashtags help you attract buyers instead of just researchers. If you make and sell wedding items, broad topic hashtags like #weddings won't be as useful to you as more specific hashtags like #weddingfashions, or #handmadeweddings.

* Use apps to find hashtags related to your niche like keywordtool.io, displaypurposes.com, skedsocial.com, hashtagify. me, or all-hashtag.com. *AutoHash* is a mobile app that analyzes your images and suggests hashtags.

* You can add up to thirty hashtags when you post or comment, but adding so many looks spammy. The fix is to add a comment and include hashtags in the comment.

* Studies show posts with multiple hashtags get twice the amount of interaction with viewers.

* Mix hashtags among your posts and comments.

* Use one of your hashtags for your Instagram name.

* Look at the posts on the most popular profiles in your niche. See hashtags you had not thought of?

* After your profile has received likes, comments, and followers over time use the "Insights" feature in your business account to discover which hashtags brought the most traffic to your Etsy store or website.

* Find keywords by starting to type in the search bar at Instagram and note the auto-complete drop-down list of popular tags. Instagram's auto-complete comes from actual searches.

* Save all your hashtags in a text file or spreadsheet. Separate them by niches, products, people, or other categories. When you need hashtags, just go to your file and copy them.

* Use hashtags used by communities related to your product's niche.

### Where to Place Hashtags

* As a sticker on your images and videos
* Your post's description
* Comments you leave
* Comments you get
* Your Instagram stories
* Your profile bio

### Tips for Posting

* When someone likes or comments on your image posts, send them a thank you. It's a natural way to start a conversation.

* If your creative muse takes a vacation, post other people's content.

* Study the posts of the most popular Instagram profiles in your niche. Look for content that attracted the most comments. This is a great way to get inspired for what you could post.

* Follow the followers of other sellers in your niche. If they appear to be frequent or recent posters, start liking their images. Many of them will follow you back.

* Follow Etsy sellers with complementary product lines to yours. Comment and like their content. Message them and see if they would like to cross-promote each other's lines.

* Post often. Uploading content twice a day has shown to increase followers. Use one of the social media scheduling tools described earlier.

* Instagram is highly social. Tagging others (adding @personsusername) can earn goodwill and increase your post comments.

### Selling from Instagram

Instagram allows shoppable posts which visitors can buy your products by clicking a button. Shoppable posts show a shopping bag icon so viewers know they can purchase directly.

Users can also click through to browse your "Shop" catalog from your Instagram profile.

* As Instagram is owned by Facebook, start the set up process on Instagram by first a Facebook Catalog in your Facebook Business Manager.

* Create a Facebook Shop. For a detailed video on setting up a Facebook Shop, see https://www.youtube.com/watch?v=jahKOMsOka0 . Or use Shopify or another multichannel listing app.

* Connect your Facebook Shop to your Instagram business account.

* Upload images to your Instagram account that you want to tag for sale.

* For a step-by-step walkthrough, see https://www.facebook.com/business/instagram/shopping/guide

### Instagram Advertising

* Like with most social platforms, you can promote your Instagram posts through paid advertising. For business accounts, the "Insights" function provides clues about which of your posts make good candidates for promoting.

* Start off with a small budget and test. Target your ad to reach followers of popular sellers in your niche.

* As with all paid promotions, include a call to action. Make it clear what you want viewers to do: visit your Etsy shop, make a purchase, sign up for your newsletter, or other action.

* Monitor your Etsy shop stats closely when you run an Instagram or other ad campaign. Your Etsy stats will tell you if you are getting traffic from Instagram or other social networks. If ads are working, increase your budget and try new audiences.

* If your ads do not result in profitable sales, stop the campaigns. Change your content, or your offer, or your audience.

# Twitter Tips

Twitter has over 300 million users who produce 500 million tweets every day. Eighty percent of Twitter users live outside the US, yet twenty-four percent of Americans use the site.

\* \* \* \* \* \*

## Etsy Likes Twitter

*Since around forty percent of Twitter users report they have bought something after viewing an influencer's tweet, it's worth including in your social media marketing mix. Etsy tweets about products their shoppers might buy. They have amassed over 2.4 million Twitter followers. Etsy seller Chanel Huston reported on Mashable.com that her sales tripled in the months after she started using Twitter.*

\* \* \* \* \* \*

### Setting Up Your Account

* As with your other social accounts, choose a username / handle or close version of your business name that helps identify your brand.
* Set up a Twitter business account (or convert your personal account) to take advantage of extra features.

### Growing Your Following

* Search Twitter for popular influencers in your niche and other sellers with products like yours. If you sell accessories, type in what kind, like "handbags", in the search bar at Twitter. com. On the sidebar, Twitter suggests "Who to Follow." As you follow some, Twitter continues to show more in your interests.
* Bloggers use Twitter to announce their newest posts. Use Twitter to find bloggers who review products like yours.
* Follow leaders in your field (those with lots of followers) and follow their followers. As long as your Tweets are helpful or entertaining, many will follow you back.
* Seek popular Twitter users in related niches. For example, if you sell repurposed clothing or accessories, identify big influencers in fashion to follow.
* When entering or starting conversations on Twitter, aim for engagement. You'll grow your influence faster with genuine connections rather than just blasting out promotional tweets.

### Tweets

* Tweet directly from Etsy when you publish a new product listing, get a five-star review, or offer a coupon. See Shop Manager > Marketing > Social media.

* Learn the best time of the day to tweet with a tool like Tweriod.com.

* Posting on Twitter teaches you how to focus your message. Tweets are limited to 280 characters.

* Tweeting is another way to engage through dialog. It's like sending brief instant messages.

* Frequent tweets generate more followers. Use social posting tools like Hootsuite or Buffer to schedule when your messages go out.

* Mix your tweet content; seven helpful or entertaining tweets for every one tweet about your products. If that feels too pushy, try ten to one (promo).

* Tweets with images get more engagement. This rule is true on most social media sites.

* Tweets with links get lots of clicks.

* Use Twitter Analytics to learn which of your tweets get the most engagement.

* Tweetdeck.twitter.com lets you manage all your Twitter activity.

### Selling from Twitter

Selling on Twitter is as simple as tweeting with a link to an item in your Etsy or other online shopping cart. However, before you start pitching everyone, create lists of potential buyers using Twitter Lists. For instance, your most important list will be previous customers.

### Hashtags

* Hashtags (putting the # sign before a keyword tag) in Twitter work like they do in Instagram.

* Using two relevant hashtags in a tweet gets more engagement.

* See the section on Instagram hashtags as the same guidelines apply on Twitter.

Like social media marketing, publicity is a way to get your message out to the audiences of others. The next chapter describes how to get publicity by getting influencers to mention, review, or recommend your indie-made products.

# CHAPTER 13

# Getting Publicity and Influencer Marketing

Publicity, or public relations (PR), is attention given to a person or product by the media. With the right pitch, your handmade product line could get mentions in popular blogs, Instagram feeds, Pinterest boards, podcasts, magazines, or other media that result in sales.

Is influencer marketing worth going after? Appearing in a magazine, popular blog, or on TV builds your brand credibility and social proof and can propel your sales to new heights.

Here you will learn how to get publicity based on your story. We'll cover:

- How to prepare before reaching out to the media
- Types of influencer media
- Where to find media contacts
- Tips for getting publicity

## How to Prepare before Reaching out to Influencers

One study showed that ninety percent of journalists begin story research by searching online. If they find you and your story is newsworthy, they will write about you.

Before you reach out to a reporter, blogger, or product reviewer, prepare an online media kit. Here is a list of what your media kit should include:

\* **Your message**. What's your story, your background, your vision/mission? You need a seven-word version, a one-paragraph version, and a longer complete bio of all you have accomplished that's relevant to your handcrafted product line.

* **A downloadable, bulleted fact sheet** of who you are, what you do, where you live, when you got started, how you make your fashion crafts, and your contact information.

* **"About me" page**. The story of your background, education, awards, and anything pertinent to your craft. Avoid listing your complete job history unless a position specifically applied to developing your side hustle.

* **High resolution, professional-looking photos of you**, you knitting, crocheting, or sewing your crafts, and several of your best-looking pieces.

* **Videos** of you making or talking about your indie designs.

* **News release** about you and your work.

* **Exhibit dates** if you have art or craft shows lined up for the coming year.

* **Previous media mentions**: interviews, articles, press clips, or reviews.

* **Awards** or competitions you have won.

* **List of ten or twelve sample questions** for an interview.

* If you have them, include jokes or **fun facts**.

* **Your contact information**.

# Types of PR

Publicity takes many forms including mention in newspapers, magazines, TV, and online media such as blogs, podcasts, videos, and social site posts.

If you make a good pitch and your photos are interesting, local newspapers, magazines, and TV affiliate stations are likely to mention you because you are part of the community. If you get written about in one or more media, mention it when pitching on other blogs and to social influencers.

### Social Influencers

Influencers on Instagram, Facebook, Twitter, Pinterest or YouTube produce content exposed to thousands—even hundreds of thousands—of followers. How do you find these opinion shapers? Social monitoring tools like <u>Heepsy.com</u> and <u>MightyScout.com</u> locate them for you. Though they are subscription services, you can sign up for a month, find lists of influencers in your genre, download the lists and have plenty of contacts to pitch.

\* \* \* \* \* \*

## The Media Loves Eco-Friendly

*Several years ago, a couple approached me for advice on growing their craft business. They sewed used inner tubes destined for landfills into fashion handbags and accessories. We came up with a news release that told their story and how they were helping save the planet. That angle got them mentioned in magazines including Rolling Stone, on radio shows including The Paul Harvey Show, numerous online blogs and even a mention on The Today Show.*

\* \* \* \* \* \*

*Bloggers Who Review Handmade Products*

Shopping bloggers review new indie-made products—some for a fee, some for a free product. Before you pitch a blogger, read their past posts and get familiar with how they've written about other products like yours.

Besides reviews, bloggers mention product giveaways or contests. If a blogger agrees to write about your items, they will include a link to your store. A contest can drive new visitors to your Etsy or online store.

The more popular the blog the more requests they get to review products. Your pitch can stand out by:
- Addressing the blogger by name
- Praising one or two of their past posts that you like
- Providing great images of your work
- Offering to link to them from your blog or social feed
- Being authentic. Tell your story. People love stories they can relate to.

The following blogs have reviewed handmade products. If one of these looks like a match for what you make, study their past reviews, send them a brief pitch, and request their product submission guidelines.

- WhoWhatWear.com/indie-fashion-brands
- Ohjoy.blogs.com
- Coolmompicks.com
- Mightygoods.com
- Weheartthis.com
- Indiefixx.com
- Tryhandmade.com
- Wickedlychic.com
- Hearthandmadeblog.com
- Mixedplateblog.com

### Newspapers and Magazines

Most major media like newspapers and magazines look for stories that inform, educate, provoke, or entertain their readers. When you can supply editors with news or stories that relate to the interests of their audiences, you have made their jobs easier. The key is pitching reporters that have covered stories like yours. Finding contact information for the media is described later in this chapter.

\* \* \* \* \* \*

## The Made Collection

*Sarah took to sewing and creating new stuff while in middle school. She made custom bags for friends while in college, which grew into a business and a line called The Made Collection. While volunteering in Africa and India, she got inspired to teach village women how to sew and create their own business. Her experiences led to opening a sewing school whose income helps fund women in poor countries.*

\* \* \* \* \* \*

# How to Pitch the Media

The job of editors, writers, reporters and producers is finding stories to develop for their audiences. They get lots of pitches from product sellers every day and reject most.

Media reporters can look at a pitch or news release and determine in seconds if it's right for their readers or viewers. The key phrase is "their readers or viewers." This is where most pitches fail. The message or product is too self-promotional or isn't a fit for their audience. If you want someone in the media to mention you, learn all you can about what stories they write about.

Start your pitch by letting the person know how you found them and why you enjoy their content. Follow with a paragraph or two and a link to a longer news release on your website's online media kit.

Your pitch should be a brief enough introduction to your story that the editor is intrigued but not overwhelmed with too much information. State a problem that your handmade item solves, like using "plarn" (repurposed plastic spun into yarn) that would otherwise add to landfills. Describe your solution. Then link readers to your website, Facebook page, or blog for more information.

Part of your story is visual, so you will want to include your best images and/or video if you have it. If the person you are pitching wants to know more, they will contact you.

## Where to Find Media Contacts

Media contacts could be writers, reporters, bloggers, producers, podcasters, and editors. There are many ways to find them.

As mentioned earlier, **Heepsy.com** and **MightyScout.com** are two of the many social listening tools offering both free and paid subscription options. Use them to find influencers by their audience, reach, and engagement.

**Google.com/alerts** programs Google to send you an alert when any news appears about "sustainable fashion" or any other topic. Look for stories covering "fashion shows" that appear in local and national publications. Make a note of the reporter or blogger's name and find their contact information.

**Twitter** helps you locate editors, producers, bloggers, and reviewers. In the search bar, type in the name of the media and hit enter. Then choose the "People" tab. For example, typing HGTV brings up show producers and reporters and what topics they cover. Also search by job title. For instance, search for "product reviewer" and start following reviewers who cover products like yours. A survey reported that forty-six percent of journalists receive story pitches through Twitter.

**Print magazine mastheads** are typically found in the first pages. It's the section that lists the publisher, editor and other staff including editors who cover specific sections like New Products, Startups, etc.

**USNPL.com** is a free-to-access directory of newspaper reporters in the US.

**HelpAReporter.com (HARO)** is a free newsletter sending out lists of media reporters looking for stories on a huge variety of topics. You can subscribe to receive one or more lists around broad topics. One topic that may be useful to indie makers is the "Giftbag" list.

The following is an example of a listing that previously showed up in my inbox from my subscribing to the HARO "Giftbag" newsletter. This request has expired so do not contact them. It's included here to give you an idea of why subscribing to this list could be useful to your business. Did I mention that HARO is free?

\* \* \* \* \* \*

## HARO Giftbag Product Requests:

*Summary: Expose Your Products to TOP producers/editors from Rachael Ray, Dr. Oz, Entrepreneur Mag (& More)*
  *Name: Michelle Pippin National Blog*
  *Category: Giftbag*
  *Media Outlet: National Blog*
  *Deadline: 7:00 PM EST - 15 June - I'm hosting*

*an event to bring 25 female thought leaders AND TOP MEDIA decision makers into the same room. List of media attending: THE Editor in Chief of Entrpreneur magazine, The top producer for Rachael Ray, the top talent finder for Dr. Oz, top producer for the Wendy Williams show, Fox Business, Fox News, CNN producer for special features, writer for Forbes magazine, and more. If you'd like to get your product in front of the right 25 (well-connected, driven, decisive and successful) women in business AND this impressive list of media outlets. THIS IS IT. There is no fee to have your products included in the bags, but if you have any questions, please direct them to ------------. Our event will be held in Midtown Manhattan and host women from all over the country.*

\* \* \* \* \* \*

## More Tips for Getting Publicity

\* Follow and read the publications, news feeds, blogs, or watch the TV shows to which you are thinking of pitching your story.

\* Target media outlets and reporters relevant to your work. If you crochet hair bows for young girls, don't contact a writer for Popular Mechanics.

\* Discover if they have reviewed businesses like yours.

\* Search for the "New Products" section of a publication. These departments are always looking for cool new stuff for their readers.

\* Pictures and videos tell stories. Reporters look for interesting visuals accompanying news releases. Got pictures of dogs wearing the cute knitted scarves you make?

\* Whenever you come out with a new product, send out a news release. Send a product sample to local newspapers and TV networks.

\* Announce any awards you have just won. Local newspapers like to feature independent businesses that receive recognition as it looks great for the community.

\* Write a story if where you work is in a historic or unusual location.

\* Take advantage of holiday gift buying. Feature editors look for stories ahead of holidays.

\* Can you relate your items to special days or months? March is National Crafts Month. Find more interesting facts about each month of the year at gone-ta-pott.com/facts-about-each-month-directory.html.

\* Donate a piece you make to a charitable cause or charity fundraiser. Send a news release to local newspapers, magazines, and TV shows with a photo of your piece.

\* Sponsor a local community event and publicize it to local newspapers.

\* Reporters are always looking for news items that tie into what's being read and talked about in the mainstream media. Can you link a popular topic to your product line?

\* At the end of your pitch to the media, link to your online media kit.

Collect any mentions of you by influencers or the media and put them in your website's media kit. If you plan to grow your brand and sell to boutiques, you'll find a portfolio of press clippings can be very persuasive when approaching stores.

When you want to scale a side hustle into a larger business, selling wholesale is the way to go. But it isn't for everyone. Keep reading to discover if building a wholesale operation is right for you.

# CHAPTER 14

# Wholesaling to Stores & Boutiques

Wholesaling means selling to boutiques, stores, and catalogs who then sell your products to their customers. At the time of this book's publication, many stores closed because of Covid. Some are re-opening.

Wholesaling allows you to grow your business by getting shops and others to sell your pieces while you stay home and focus on making them. The tips here will help you build relationships with one or as many store owners as you can handle.

Though the potential for scaling your business upward through selling wholesale is huge, there is a price that comes with expansion. It means you will spend increasingly more of your time managing people you hire and train to help you and less time making products. It means double-checking each item before shipping to make sure every piece was made with attention to details. It means calculating profit margins to the penny.

In this chapter, we will look at what it means to get involved in selling to stores like:

- Preparing to sell wholesale
- Finding wholesale buyers
- Working with stores and boutiques
- Overlooked retail outlets

## Preparing to Sell Wholesale

### Know Your Profit Margin

In Chapter 4 on pricing, you learned how to determine your profit margin and whether you can sell your items wholesale.

Normally, if your production cost is one-fourth (or lower) of the store's retail price, you will make a profit wholesaling. If a store's retail price is $25, your cost should be $6.25 or lower.

Stores typically mark an item's price at two and a half times its cost. For example, if a store buys an item for $10, they will retail it for $25.

### Your Production Capacity

How many items can you produce in one week? Is your production consistent and predictable? Stores like to offer their clientele new work regularly. Can you envision coming up with fresh product ideas two to three times a year?

### Establish Your Terms

When a store buyer asks your terms for wholesale accounts, you need a handout with something like the following:

\*   \*   \*   \*   \*   \*

## Example: Wholesale Terms

*Net 30 terms available with approval upon your third order. Opening orders are prepaid via Visa, Mastercard, AmEx, Discover or PayPal or company check (with seven business day delay). Orders ship insured within three days via UPS or Priority Mail from Santa Fe, NM to addresses throughout US. Opening minimum order: $300, minimum reorder: $150. Prepaid orders of $250+ get free shipping to US addresses. Products are sold on a non-returnable basis. While rare, any defective merchandise may be returned at my expense within 14 days of delivery.*

\*   \*   \*   \*   \*   \*

### What Store Buyers Like

Be professional. Your business can be new but should show signs you are serious about it. At the minimum, store buyers expect you to have a brand or business name, wholesale terms, catalog sheets of your work, and an artist's story.

It's also helpful to have a portfolio you can show them of your work, other boutiques carrying your line (not in their immediate area), and any media coverage you may have gotten. Imagine walking into a boutique with a handful of magazine or blogger article reprints featuring their review of your product.

## Finding Wholesale Buyers

Visit stores: Ever walked by a shop you would love to have your pieces in? Just go in and talk to the owner, unless the person is with a customer. In which case, quietly wait until they are free. Ask if you can make an appointment to show them your portfolio. If they aren't busy, they may want to look right then.

If you make clothing or accessories, always wear something you make!

\*  \*  \*  \*  \*  \*

### It's Okay to Walk into a Store to Pitch Your Line

*Kendra Scott started her line from home with $500. She pitched her pieces to local boutiques going door to door and meeting buyers. Her designs became so loved they made it to the runway for an Oscar de la Renta show. Her lines grew to include home accessories and beauty products. Kendra eventually opened her own store, then another and another. In 2016, she sold part of her company to Warren Buffett's Berkshire Partners at a valuation of $1 billion.*

\*  \*  \*  \*  \*  \*

Locate indie boutiques by state:
- elle.com/fashion/g8016/50-states-of-shopping-best-boutiques-in-america/
- garmentory.com/sale/boutiques
- vox.com/2016/10/5/13149580/

> online-shopping-cool-indie-boutiques
- independent.co.uk/extras/indybest/us/best-online-clothes-shops-women-fashion-asos-workout-desig-ner-a8705896.html

LinkedIn.com: Locate buyers through LinkedIn. The following results are from searches made on LinkedIn.com:
- 14,000 "accessories buyer"
- 2,200 "wearable art gallery"
- 9,500 "apparel buyer"
- 5,900 "boutique owner"
- 232 "boutique buyer"
- 4,200 "bridal registry"

Wholesale buying portals. The websites below act as online portals where independent retail store buyers can purchase directly from makers. Each site has its own terms for listing products:
- Stockabl.com
- Tundra.com
- Faire.com
- Indieme.com
- LAShowroom.com
- Wholesaleinabox.com
- Trouva.com (UK)

At craft shows, store buyers find you: I have displayed my handmade accessory lines at highly competitive craft shows, some attended by hundreds of thousands of shoppers. At the better shows, I typically pick up one new store account just from buyers or owners shopping at such events for new products.

## Working with Stores

When working with stores face-to-face, the checklist here will increase your success:

\* Be on time for appointments. Don't show irritation if they are running late and need you to wait a bit.

* Have line sheets, price lists, product pages and business cards with you.

* Find an attractive bag or cases for carrying samples into stores. Cardboard boxes and garbage bags present a poor image.

* Show interest in the owner's store. They will appreciate compliments.

* Ask questions. Store buyers are usually happy to share advice with product makers. Ask them what their customers are buying this year, which colors are in, or how often they like to see new product lines.

* Not every store buyer you approach will buy. If you get a "no" be graceful and ask if the buyer has any suggestions about how to improve your work.

* Stay in touch with your buyers. They carry many items from many makers. They could run out of one of your products and only remember to order when you check in to learn how they are doing.

* It is acceptable in wholesale to ask for payment at the time of a store buyer's first order; some makers ask for payment for the first two orders. After the initial purchase(s), be prepared to extend credit to your store account for thirty days. This is commonly called net 30.

* If a buyer isn't pre-paying, ask for a purchase order number at the time they place an order. A purchase order is your proof that they placed an order.

* What do you do after you have extended credit and the account does not pay? Remain calm. Avoid calling the store and angrily demanding payment. Remind them politely that you cannot ship more products until they pay the outstanding invoices. If they haven't paid in ninety days, send a more strongly worded letter that asks for them to take care of the past due bills before you turn to a collection agency.

* Most shipping services like UPS, FedEx Ground, and the U.S. Postal Service provide tracking numbers when you ship through them. This is your record that the buyers received the packages, in case there's any dispute.

* Stores usually pay shipping charges. Add this amount on to the invoice when billing.

* Encourage buyers to pay up front; offer free shipping when they pay at the time they order. This is a big saving for them and many will jump on it. Know your profit margins and determine if you can afford to offer this perk.

* If you plan on doing craft shows in the same cities where you have store accounts, make your retail prices the same as the stores'.

* Set up a secure shopping cart to process wholesale orders online. This makes it easy for your store buyers to order and speeds getting payments to you.

\* \* \* \* \* \*

## Sometimes Getting Publicity Doesn't Work Out

*Sarah Oliver began knitting handbags as gifts and selling them here and there at trunk shows at friends' parties. To increase production, she went to retirement homes. Employing 70-to-90-year-old retirees she called "The Purlettes," she knew that seniors often found themselves undervalued. She wanted to change that by paying the seniors by the bag to make them for her as independent contractors. Sarah's story and handbags were featured in Oprah Magazine, Forbes, Inc, and on Shark Tank. Unfortunately, the Department of Labor took notice and shut down her business, saying that the retirees making the inventory weren't legally independent contractors and the company wasn't paying them an hourly wage.*

\* \* \* \* \* \*

## Overlooked Retailers for Handmade Goods

Retail stores and boutiques aren't the only outlets for fashion crafts. Depending on what you make, check out these alternative markets:

* **Businesses, organizations, and individuals hire interior designers** to arrange their living or business spaces and find

items to place there. Get your products in front of home and office interior buyers at houzz.com and artfulhome.com.

* **Gift shops** at airports, hotels, museums, hospitals, and marinas carry handmade items. Locate gift shops in the US at gift-shops.regionaldirectory.us and in the UK: directory.independent.co.uk/gift-shops/in/uk.

* **Beauty salons and spas** partner with jewelry and accessory makers. Find them at spaindex.com.

* **Campgrounds** at national parks and tourist areas usually have gift shops. See reserveamerica.com/campgroundDirectory.do.

* **Mail-order catalogs** can also be a market for your handmade products. One of the most popular for handmade items is the *Sundance Catalog*, started by Robert Redford. Neiman Marcus publishes a holiday catalog that showcases fine handcrafted items. *The Vermont Country Store* and *Coldwater Creek* catalog offers handmade interior accessories and gift ideas.

The marketing tactics we've covered in this book can help get your products in front of more buyers. But even if someone doesn't buy from you the first time they find you, capturing their e-mail address gives you the ability to send a newsletter or follow-up messages with special offers and updates about your business. The next chapter teaches you how to grow and follow up with a mailing list of followers.

# CHAPTER 15

# Your Customer Mailing List

A mailing list makes it easy to market to people or stores who have bought from you before. As mentioned in the chapter on social media, no matter how large your online following, you don't own them. Your follower list belongs to Facebook, Instagram, Pinterest, or other site. If something happens to your account or to the site, you lose them.

With an e-mail list, you can contact your customers on a regular basis. A mailing list is a valuable asset. A study by the US Consumer Affairs Department says for every marketing dollar you spend to keep a current customer, you'll spend five dollars to get a new one.

Building a craft business with staying power isn't just about making sales, it's about creating lasting relationships. This chapter explores the many ways to stay connected with your customers and coax them into lifetime loyalty. Learn the importance of:
- Capturing and working with e-mails
- Excuses to follow up
- How to treat customers well

## Growing an E-mail List

When you make a sale, ask your customer if she would like to be on your mailing list. Many will say yes because they just found something from a seller they like. Take advantage of their enthusiasm. Even when a shopper shows interest but doesn't buy, the next best thing is to get them on your list.

As mentioned earlier, when promoting on social media sites like Instagram, Facebook, Twitter, Pinterest, or elsewhere, capturing e-mail addresses should be one of your goals.

*Tools for capturing and managing customer e-mails*

The following tools help you capture e-mails and manage your mailing list. You can create a series of autoresponders or send out a special offer or let your customers know about a new product you are launching: Aweber.com, Mailchimp.com, Get-response.com, and Convertkit.com.

These tools also allow you to personalize e-mails to get a better response. An example is an e-mail addressed to a person by first name in the e-mail subject area and with the person's name included in the body text of the e-mail. One study showed that personalized e-mails generated over 400 percent more sales on average than non-personalized e-mails.

*Five tips for e-mail:*

1. Improve your response rates by letting people know in the e-mail subject area and in the opening text of the e-mail the reason you are writing to them.
2. People are busy, so get to the point of your message right away, whether it's letting them know about a special saving, a new product offer, or a craft show you will be exhibiting at in their area.
3. Remind customers of who you are and your previous relationship with them.
4. Send e-mail only to those people who have given you permission.
5. When someone asks to be removed from your list, do it. Avoid getting pegged as a spammer. You can lose your account and face criminal charges if found to be in violation of the CanSpam Act.

## Excuses to Follow Up

The average cost of getting new customers is six to ten times the cost of staying in touch with current ones. When you can't think of a good reason to reconnect with your contacts, here are thirty excuses to reach out and remind people of you.

- Thank someone for visiting your booth at an event
- Thank your customer after each sale
- Announce a special sale
- Announce a contest
- Announce a new product release
- Send a product sample
- Advise about discontinued items
- Send a gift
- Learn if a customer got their order
- Learn if a customer got your letter, flyer, or communication
- Send a newsletter
- Send a postcard or flyer with a schedule of your upcoming shows and exhibits
- Send a product tip sheet
- Send a product catalog
- Ask for a referral
- Thank someone for a referral
- Offer a coupon or incentive to get customers to come back
- Offer to link to someone's website from your own
- Make your customer feel important by creating a preferred customer offering
- Send a news clipping or copy of an article appearing about you
- Share ideas for holiday gifts and special occasions
- Send interesting facts about the piece a customer bought
- Seek a host for a home party or trunk show
- Thank someone for sponsoring a home party or trunk show
- Send a customer survey asking for feedback on how you measured up for service and quality of product
- Encourage more orders by sending testimonials from satisfied customers
- Send cards celebrating holidays other than Christmas—like Mother's Day, Graduation, Thanksgiving and Valentine's Day

- Make amends for a mistake you made
- Link your products to a recognized month. As mentioned earlier, January is special because it is: Chilly Month, National Eye Care Month, National Soup Month, Whale-Watching Month, National Egg Month, National Wheat Bread Month, and much more.

Create a follow-up calendar scheduling the above action steps so you have a plan for staying in touch.

\* \* \* \* \* \*

## Following Through, Following Up

*Walking down the outdoor mall in downtown Boulder, CO, I was on a road trip searching for shops to sell my handwoven ruanas and shawls to.*

*A gift store that sold Southwestern style gifts caught my eye. I went in and saw a nice collection of moderately expensive arts and crafts but no weaving. I was about to leave when I suddenly thought to ask the owner about carrying my work. Since I lived and worked near Santa Fe and her shop's theme was Southwestern, maybe she would see a fit for her clientele.*

*The owner asked to see samples. I went to my car and brought back everything I had—a dozen pieces. She took them all on consignment.*

*When I returned to New Mexico, life got busy again. I was weaving at least forty hours a week making inventory for upcoming shows and filling wholesale orders to ten other stores.*

*About six weeks go by and I finally remember the Boulder shop. I phone and the owner says, "I'm so glad you called. I just put a check in the mail. We sold everything. Ship me more."*

*I'm so glad I followed through with my impulse to talk with her that first meeting. Over time, her store became one of my best accounts.*

\* \* \* \* \* \*

## Treat Customers Well

Customers talk to their friends about their shopping experiences, especially when they feel they've been treated badly. On average, an unhappy customer tells seven to fifteen others about their negative experience.

Customers are more likely to leave a negative review when they have a bad experience than take time to write a positive review. Since reviews are the fuel for online sales, make it a priority to fix customer issues immediately to avoid getting bad reviews.

Customers are five times more likely to stop doing business with someone because of mistreatment than because of any other reason.

Building and maintaining your customer list is one of many important practices covered in this book.

When things are selling and you find your business growing, remember to keep an eye on the bottom line. The next chapter gives you several ways to boost your profit margins.

CHAPTER 16

# Increasing Profits

As explained in Chapter 4 on pricing, profit margin is the difference between your costs and your revenues. Without healthy margins, your venture can't thrive or grow. Successful businesses, even those that are profitable, remain on the lookout for ways to improve.

There are two places in your business to look at where you can improve profits. You can (1) lower costs and/or (2) raise prices. This chapter gives tips for doing both.

## Get More Done While Reducing Your Labor Costs

Production time improves with practice. After weaving (and simultaneously struggling to learn sewing and knitting) for several years, I thought I had reached a peak for how fast I could produce my pieces.

But when I searched Google for production weaving tips, I found a list of 100 ways to weave better and faster. These tips saved me five minutes in one step, another saved ten minutes. That may not sound like much, but every minute you save to produce your products, the higher your profit margins.

The following are a few of the resources I found when searching for speeding up production of various textile crafts:

**Sewing:** thesprucecrafts.com/sewing-tips-4162915

**Knitting:** knitom.com/25-knitting-tips-better-knitter/

**Weaving:** peggyosterkamp.com/100-great-weaving-tips/

**Quilting:** seasonedhomemaker.com/how-to-finish-more-quilts-with-these-time-saving-tips/

**Crocheting:** mybluprint.com/article/how-to-crochet-faster

**Needlepoint:** needlenthread.com/2015/10/10-tips-for-quicker-easier-stitching.html

For more time-saving ideas, search Google for "_____ production tips," filling in the blank with the skill you want to get faster at.

As your fashion craft business grows and you outsource production, teach your employees or independent contractors how you want your items made using faster and smarter techniques.

## Save Money Lowering Your Material Costs

I am always on the lookout for ways to lower my material costs. Over the years, the following tips have saved me a bundle:

**Buying bargain supplies on eBay:** Almost every day, eBay shows new listings of wholesale craft supplies. Go to the "Crafts" category and then "Wholesale Lots" or search for "quilting supplies" or "knitting yarns" or whatever you need for your specific craft materials. Look for sellers who have positive feedback and deals that include free shipping.

**Buying direct from manufacturers:** Save money by buying your materials in bulk. Check out: wholesale craft supplies at wholesalecentral.com/Crafts-Supplies.html.

Also, **locate manufacturers of craft supplies through the Thomas Register**; it lists most major manufacturers by product. Your library should have a copy in the reference section or see: thomasnet.com. Note that most manufacturers require a resale number and may only sell to you if they think you are a production studio or retail store. Contact manufacturers as if you were already in business as a retail store. You will need a sales tax ID, business stationery, business cards, and the names of other major suppliers you buy from.

**Buying from other countries**: You may find cheap sources in Asia and other countries. The most popular site for manufacturers of supplies in other countries is Alibaba.com. However, before you order, learn if there will be tariffs or import duties on what you buy from overseas.

**Sales at your favorite retailer or Hobby Lobby, Michaels and Joann's**: Get the mobile apps for these major retailers as they regularly send out discount codes.

Google the phrase "**wholesale craft supplies**" substituting your media for craft; for instance, bead artists search for "wholesale bead supplies." I listed this method last because there are many websites purporting to sell wholesale to the public, though most just use the terminology as a marketing ploy. But I have found legitimate wholesale suppliers after sorting through the less reliable listings.

## Raising Your Prices

Makers just starting to sell their work typically under-price their products thinking they will attract more buyers. But in the handmade marketplace, lowering prices more often lowers the perceived value and causes shoppers to turn away.

Price is not the top buying criteria in the handmade marketplace, except where there are many competitors for low-dollar items like T-shirts. What is true more often is that the quality of your work, how-when-where you display it, your packaging, and your artist's story can positively increase your sales.

Below are things you can do to raise the perceived value, which will allow you to increase your prices and boost your sales.

**\* Raise the price until sales drop.** Shoppers of handmade items look at an item's price tag and decide about the item's value. If the price is too low, a shopper thinks the item is inferior. Many makers, including myself, have found that raising an item's price boosts sales. The way to test this is to take an item that is selling and raise the price a little. Keep raising prices every few weeks until sales drop off. Then go back to the last price where sales were steady. Test your item's ceiling price at craft shows or online on Etsy or Amazon. When selling wholesale to stores, rely on the store owner's recommendations because they know their clientele.

* **Tell them it's handmade.** State it in your marketing messages. When selling at events in your state, add "Handmade in _____(your state)."

* **Display fashion crafts as if they were art.** When doing events that allow for electricity, use spotlights aimed on your top-selling pieces. Hang items along a backdrop wall or pro-panel wall, as if they were in a gallery. I found that when I set up my craft show display to look my store walls, shoppers appreciated my work more and did not hesitate to buy as I was testing my optimum price.

* **Display your story.** Stories add a human element while enhancing perceived value. Write about how you got into your craft and where you work. Explain what went on behind the scenes to produce an item. Describe your personal journey or evolution with your skill as a designer.

*_**Improve your finishing touches.**_ Adding finishing touches to your indie-made crafts improves their perceived value. A friend took a plain weave sweater and then added trim from the cut-off warp ends and strung the yarns with assorted beads and baubles. The sweater that might have brought $150 as it was sold for $350 after the extra finishing.

* **Make Earth-friendly products.** If you use environmentally friendly materials, use words in your product signage and descriptions to remind shoppers that your products are eco-friendly or sustainable (only when any of these are true); multiple surveys report shoppers will pay more for environmentally friendly products (Fortune).

* **Use eye-catching, eco-friendly packaging.** Use biodegradable or recycled packaging like branded boxes, ribbons, or wrapping. Shoppers often buy a product's package as much as the contents and they have become increasingly conscious of the environmental impact of their purchases.

* **Personalize the product.** Customers expect to pay more to have a personalized gift they can give to someone special. The number of shopper searches for personalized handmade gifts grew over 22% on Etsy in 2019. Raise your prices if you can offer customization.

**\* Offer free shipping.** Survey after survey reports that the number one thing shoppers want when shopping online is free shipping. Eighty-eight percent of Amazon shoppers reported that free shipping draws them to shop there. On my Etsy store, offering free shipping boosted my sales. And yes, I raised my product prices to cover my mailing costs.

We covered a lot of material in this book. I hope it's given you ideas for growing your business. The last chapter highlights the more important take-aways that will help your handmade products sell better..

# CHAPTER 17

# Key Take-Aways

Over the years, my fiber crafts business has grown on four fronts: (1) art/craft fairs, (2) online on Etsy, and Handmade on Amazon, (3) my gallery-gift shop in a popular tourist location, and (4) selling wholesale to other stores. In all these different markets, I focused on cultivating relationships with customers. This has led to loads of repeat business.

My handmade business began like many artistic enterprises—as a risky venture. But my faith in myself grew along with sales. When things didn't go right, it was usually because I did something other than the recommendations on the list below.

Your business evolves as you gain confidence and gather feedback.

Expect your plan to change with circumstances. Every adjustment to my plans I made along the way had a cost. And, most of the time, a corresponding reward.

Not everything in my business has always gone smoothly. One of the most useful skills I've learned is managing my reactivity. Stuff happens. I get over it, or better yet, don't let events trigger negative emotions.

The best approach for any business owner is to apply the scientific method: theory—test—measure result—repeat if warranted and drop what doesn't work.

Based on my testing and measuring over many years, here are the take-aways I recommend you pay close attention to if you want to grow a successful handmade products business:

**1. Choose products to make that are in demand.** Make your own creative version of a trendy product.

**2. Trust your creativity, but test the marketplace** before investing heavily in a new idea. Remember this saying from the Middle East: "Trust in God, but tie your camel first."

**3. Don't let competition intimidate you.** There wouldn't be other sellers unless there was a demand. If I had let concerns about competition stop me, my handmade scarf line would never have seen the light of day.

**4. Know your production costs.** Do the math. Numbers don't lie. You have to make a profit to sustain any venture, especially if you plan to scale up by selling wholesale.

**5. If your profit margin is too low, increase your item's perceived value** so you can raise your prices. Price your items according to how much shoppers will pay.

**6. Photograph your products** as if they would appear on the cover of *Family Circle* or *Martha Stewart* magazines. Don't pinch pennies when it comes to photos. Use lifestyle images of people wearing your product.

**7. Position handmade items in front of handmade buyers.** Buy handmade is a movement not just a passing trend.

**8. Display and package your items as if you are already a successful brand**. Perception is everything in retail merchandising.

**9. Scale up by selling wholesale** or selling at more places online. There are only so many craft shows a person can do. If you want to grow, you can gradually get more and more store accounts or increase your online sales and hire help for increasing production.

**10. Listen to your customers**. Their comments will inform you what you ought to make and how you should package and display your lines.

**11. Follow your passion.** I absolutely love making my artful scarves and my customers tell me they love wearing them. When you love what you do, new opportunities open up to you. You persist in the face of obstacles. You have a business and a life.

If you really want to thrive with your handmade products business, consistently work to improve the eleven core elements above.

Success and failure are just labels.

Remember to have fun. Enjoy life. You *can* play for a living.

See opportunities everywhere. Or remain a victim of your circumstances.

I've been in both places and I know how challenging staying positive can be. But **thinking positive** is the twelfth key take-away to making everything else in this book work for you.

For a book I wrote in the global best-selling *Guerrilla Marketing* series, I interviewed twenty indiduals who had made at least a million dollars (some much more) in direct selling. Though each had built their business a different way, they all shared the same important advice: ditch negative thinking, as it's the only thing stopping you from achieving your dreams.

### You can do it!

# Images That Sell

Great photos convert online shoppers into buyers. And posters with images of people using or holding your product can boost sales at art and craft fairs.

The six types of product images that can help your sales:

1. Product-only images with white background for online store listings (required when selling on Amazon). Etsy images don't have to have a white background, but studies show they improve online sales.

2. How-it's-made images. Pictures of you making your products. Tell your story through photos.

3. Step-by-step instructional images where a person in the photo shows how to use a product, if applicable.

4. Lifestyle images showing people in real-life poses enjoying your item. If you can get them, use images of real customers (who have given permission) using your products.

5. Jury images to submit when applying to arts and crafts fairs.

6. Pictures of you to accompany your artist's story in your promotional materials and your social media profiles.

## Learning photography

If you are on a tight budget or you just want to do your own photography, the following sites offer tutorials:

- join.shawacademy.com/online-photography-course
- alison.com/tag/photography
- youtube.com/user/tutvid/playlists
- bit.ly/PHLearnVids (Photoshop tutorials)

# Finding photographers

Commercial product photographers can cost hundreds of dollars. You pay for copyrights as well as photos. Though you get great pics, you may not have the funds to invest so much money starting out. Cheaper alternatives:

- At Fiverr.com search for "product photography" to find affordable providers. Copyright is included in the fees. Look for providers with positive reviews and many completed gigs.
- Another source for finding photographers is Etsy.com. Type in the search bar "product photography" for thousands of results. Most services are for product images only, not models. If your product needs a model, expect to pay more.
- Also search for "mockup" on Etsy for thousands of examples of products in lifestyle settings.
- CreativeMarket.com and DesignCuts.com offer a large collection of mockups for simulating your product image in a lifestyle setting.

For more craft photography tips, see the resources at: handmadeology.com/big-list-of-product-photography-tips/ and the book *Photographing Arts, Crafts & Collectibles* by Steve Meltzer.

# International List of Craft Shows and Events

F ind events to display your fashion crafts according to your location. The more competitive (popular and well-attended) events have cut-off dates, so apply early.

**US & Canada**
- zapplication.org
- art-linx.com
- artfaircalendar.com
- festivalnet.com

**UK**
- craftyfoxmarket.co.uk
- handmadeinbritain.co.uk
- designersmakers.com
- 10times.com/london-uk/arts-crafts
- UKcraftfairs.com
- artfaircalendar.com
- prima.co.uk/leisure/events/a39073/best-craft-festivals-in-the-uk/
- renegadecraft.com/city/london

**Europe**
- artfaircalendar.com/art_fair/european-eu-uk-germany-france-art-shows.html
- Across Europe, open-air markets centrally located to attract tourist traffic are almost everywhere, even in smaller cities.

### Australia
- craftevents.com.au
- expertiseevents.com.au
- artfaircalendar.com
- sydneycraftweek.com
- India and Asia
- artfaircalendar.com/art_fair/asia-japan-hong-kong-korea-art-fairs.html

### International
- makerfaire.com
- Open-air markets are in most cities in Asia and India, as in Europe.

# International List of E-Commerce Markets

Etsy.com accepts payments from the following countries: Australia, Austria, Belgium, Bulgaria, Canada, Croatia, Cyprus, Czech Republic, Denmark, Estonia, Finland, France, Germany, Greece, Hong Kong, Hungary, Ireland, Italy, Latvia, Lithuania, Luxembourg, Malta, the Netherlands, New Zealand, Norway, Poland, Portugal, Romania, Singapore, Slovakia, Slovenia, Spain, Sweden, Switzerland, the United Kingdom, the United States

Amazon handmade also allows sellers to reach international customers.

### US & Canada

- etsy.com
- amazon.com/Handmade/
- artfire.com
- zibbet.com
- bonanza.com
- artfulhome.com
- ecrater.com
- houzz.com
- makersmarket.us
- uncommongoods.com
- icraftgifts.com
- latitudesdecor.com

## UK

- thefuturekept.com
- folksy.com
- madebyhandonline.com
- misi.co.uk
- miratis.com
- designersmakers.com
- designnation.co.uk
- aerende.co.uk
- personalise.co.uk
- thecraftersbarn.co.uk
- notonthehighstreet.com
- rebelsmarket.com
- artsthread.com
- affordablebritishart.co.uk
- art2arts.co.uk
- artclickireland.com

## Europe

- artbaazar.com
- artebooking.com
- zet.gallery

## Australia

- madeit.com.au
- stateoftheartgallery.com.au
- artloversaustralia.com.au
- artpharmacy.com.au

## India and Asia

- melaartisans.com
- artisera.com
- artzyme.com

## International

- artsyshark.com/sell-art-online-directory/

# About the Author

James Dillehay is a fiber craft artisan, former gallery owner, and author of fifteen books. He's sold his work at competitive juried shows in the US, wholesale to galleries and boutiques from Manhattan to the Grand Canyon, and online at Etsy, Ebay, and Amazon.

James has been interviewed in *The Wall Street Journal Online, Yahoo Finance, Bottom Line Personal, Family Circle, The Crafts Report, Working Mothers, Entrepreneur Radio, HGTV's The Carol Duvall Show*, and more.

He has developed and presented crafts marketing programs for the University of Alaska, Northern New Mexico Community College, Bootcamp for Artists and Craftspeople, and The Learning Annex.

He currently lives, writes, and creates cool stuff from a studio he built himself (and it doesn't leak) next to a national forest in New Mexico.

## Resources

Access the resources and downloads described in this book at: **https://craftmarketer.com/book-resources/**

## Courses

**W**ant more in-depth training on growing your handmade products business? As a fiber craft artisan featured in *The Wall Street Journal, Yahoo Finance,* and *Entrepreneur Radio*, marketing genius James Dillehay's thirty+ years of experience has made him a master of turning small projects into six-figure enterprises.

To learn when the next couse opens, get on James' free announcement list. You'll stay informed about what's trending now and what's coming in the world of marketing your handmade products. Subscribe at: **Craftmarketer.com/newsletter/**

\* \* \*

Please take a moment to leave your thoughts about this book in a review where you bought your copy. I read all reviews to learn how I can improve the content before publishing a revision. Thank you!

The question I get asked most is "how much should I charge for my craftwork?" Without a smart pricing strategy, it's almost impossible to succeed in the handmade marketplace.

Problem solved with the book: ***How to Price Crafts and Things You Make to Sell***—formulas and successful craft business ideas for pricing on Etsy and selling to stores, at craft shows and everywhere else.

It may well be the most useful guide you own for your maker business.

**<u>Buy on Amazon now!</u>**

Made in United States
Orlando, FL
24 November 2021

10702666R00078